love and some verses

love and some verses

A COLLECTION OF LYRICS, PHOTOS, ART, AND EPHEMERA FROM IRON & WINE

SAM BEAM

weldonowen

SAN RAFAEL · LOS ANGELES · LONDON

Contents

The Creek Drank the Cradle
Commentary — 6

About a Bruise — 9
All in Good Time — 10
An Angry Blade — 13
Angels Go Home — 14
Anyone's Game — 15
Arms of a Thief — 16
Autumn Town Leaves — 19
Baby Center Stage — 20
Bag of Cats — 22
Belated Promise Ring — 23
Beneath the Balcony — 25
Beyond the Fence — 26
Big Burned Hand — 28
Bird Stealing Bread — 29
Biting Your Tail — 30
The Bitter Suite — 33
Bitter Truth — 34
Black Candle — 37
Boy with a Coin — 38
Burn That Broken Bed — 41
Call It Dreaming — 42
Call Your Boys — 46
Calm on the Valley — 48
Carousel — 49
Carried Home — 50
Caught in the Briars — 53

Our Endless Numbered Days
Commentary — 54

Cinder and Smoke — 56
Claim Your Ghost — 58
Cold Town — 59
Communion Cups and
    Someone's Coat — 60
Cutting It Close — 63
Dead Man's Will — 64

Dearest Forsaken — 65
The Desert Babbler — 66
The Devil Never Sleeps — 68
Dirty Dream — 71
Each Coming Night — 72
Eden — 74
Elizabeth — 75

Woman King
Commentary — 76

Evening on the Ground
    (Lilith's Song) — 79
Everyone's Summer
    of '95 — 80
Ex-Lover Lucy Jones — 81
Faded from the Winter — 82
Father Mountain — 84
Fever Dream — 85
Flightless Bird,
    American Mouth — 86
Follow the Water — 88
Freckled Girl — 89
Free Until They Cut
    Me Down — 90
Freedom Hangs
    Like Heaven — 91
Friends They Are Jewels — 93
Glad Man Singing — 94
God Made the
    Automobile — 96
Godless Brother in Love — 97
Grace for Saints
    and Ramblers — 98
Grass Widows — 101
Gray Stables — 102
Half Moon — 104
Halfway to Richmond — 105

In the Reins
Commentary — 106

He Lays in the Reins — 108
Hearts Walk Anywhere — 109
Hickory — 111
A History of Lovers — 112
Homeward, These
    Shoes — 113
House by the Sea — 116
In Your Own Time — 117
Innocent Bones — 118
Jesus the Mexican Boy — 119
Jezebel — 120
John's Glass Eye — 124
Joy — 125
Judgement — 127

The Shepherd's Dog
Commentary — 128

Kicking the Old Rain — 130
Kingdom of the
    Animals — 132
Last Night — 133
Last of Your Rock 'n'
    Roll Heroes — 135
Lean into the Light — 136
Lion's Mane — 138
Loaning Me Secrets — 139
Loretta — 140
Loud as Hope — 141
Love and Some Verses — 142
Lovesong of the Buzzard — 145
Lovers' Revolution — 146
Low Light Buddy
    of Mine — 149
Me and Lazarus — 150
Milkweed — 153

Minor Piano Keys	154
Miss Bottom of the Hill	156

Kiss Each Other Clean
Commentary 160

Monkeys Uptown	163
Morning	164
Muddy Hymnal	165
My Lady's House	166
My Side of the Road	167
Naked as We Came	168
New Mexico's No Breeze	170
Next to Paradise	171
The Night Descending	173
No Moon	174
On Your Wings	175
Our Light Miles	176
Pagan Angel and a Borrowed Car	177
Passing Afternoon	178
Peace Beneath the City	179
Postcard	180
Prison on Route 41	182
Promise What You Will	183
Promising Light	184
Quarters in a Pocket	187
Rabbit Will Run	188
Radio War	191
Red Dust	192
Resurrection Fern	193
Right for Sky	194
The Rooster Moans	197
Sacred Vision	198
The Sea and the Rhythm	199
Serpent Charmer	200
Show Him the Ground	202
Sing Song Bird	203

Ghost on Ghost
Commentary 204

Singers and the Endless Song	206
Sinning Hands	207
Sixteen, Maybe Less	208
Slow Black River	209
Sodom, South Georgia	210
Someday the Waves	212
Song in Stone	213
Southern Anthem	214
Straight and Tall	215
Stranger Lay Beside Me	216

Beast Epic / Weed Garden
Commentary 218

Summer Clouds	220
Summer in Savannah	222
Sundown (Back in the Briars)	223
Sunset Soon Forgotten	224
Swans and the Swimming	225
Sweet Talk	227
Taken by Surprise	228
Talking to Fog	230
Tears That Don't Matter	232
Teeth in the Grass	235
This Solemn Day	236
Thomas County Law	237

"The Trapeze Swinger"
Commentary 238

The Trapeze Swinger	240
Tree by the River	243
The Truest Stars We Know	244
Two Hungry Blackbirds	245

Upward Over the Mountain	246
Valentine	248
Wade Across the Water	249
Walking Far from Home	250
Waves of Galveston	252
Weary Memory	253

Years to Burn
Commentary 256

What Heaven's Left	258
What Hurts Worse	259
White Tooth Man	260
Why Hate the Winter	261
The Wind Is Low	262
Winter Prayers	263
Wolves (Song of the Shepherd's Dog)	264
Woman King	266
Years to Burn	267

Light Verse
Commentary 268

Yellow Jacket	272
You Never Know	273
Your Fake Name Is Good Enough for Me	274
Your Sly Smile	276

Index by Album	278
About the Author	283
Song Credits	284

Album Commentaries by Sam Beam with Anders Smith Lindall

The Creek Drank the Cradle

I was always way into music. A capital F kind of fan, the way creative types can often be. But I never really thought of writing songs as a thing that people *did*. Songs were just something you'd listen to and live with. In the mid-nineties, when I was about twenty-five, I was in film school in Tallahassee, and there was a bunch of recording equipment around. I don't know what clicked in my brain, but I just sort of said, "Let's try it!" That's honestly all it took for me to get hooked.

I always liked making things, and art was a big part of my life before that. But that was visual art-making, or writing screenplays. Being able to record songs turned music into shaping something, like I would do with visual art—making marks and adjusting and editing and developing a thing—instead of just an inspiration that came and disappeared. Pretty soon I was spending a lot of my spare time writing songs. I can't say I thought of it as starting down any kind of path, only a new thing that I enjoyed.

I was sharing a house with classmates, and it was gross. We'd smoke in there, and we never did the dishes. Pretty typical student bachelor pad situation, but we were working hard. I loved film school, but any spare moment I wasn't working on a film, I would be at the house recording a song. You can hear some of them now on *Archive Series Vol. 5: Tallahassee Recordings*.

After school, I moved to Miami to work. It was a huge culture shock. Film school had put all this wind in my sails, and then, like lots of people, I hit reality. I didn't know anybody, and even though I was working pretty consistently on movies and commercials, filmmaking wasn't feeding my spirit the way I'd hoped it would. It was demoralizing. I wouldn't have admitted it at the time, but I felt like the dream was over. Up to that point, I'd given all my heart energy to filmmaking. Now, even though I was working a lot, it just wasn't feeding my creative side. It might sound impatient or even selfish, but I'm an artist, and we all want to put our energy into something that feeds us back. More and more, as the months passed, all of my energy went into songs.

I lived with a roommate from school, but I spent a lot of time alone in our apartment, which was close to the beach. This whole record sounds like that apartment to me. Miami is an exciting place, but I was feeling out of place and missing home. A lot of the imagery was about nostalgia, both real and romanticized. Moving away from the comforts of familiarity, wanting to create something for myself, and feeling that work was pushing me away and sending me into the bedroom to write and be rewarded there—those are the reasons this stuff was made.

I grew up around Columbia, South Carolina. Throughout the nineties, when I was in school, when I would come back home and hang out with my friends, we'd sit around and listen to music, talk about music, get really excited about music. Ben Bridwell, who people know from Band of Horses, was in that circle. He had some friends that he was playing with, a group called Carissa's Weird. And I thought that was so cool. He had a band! And they'd moved to Seattle!

By 2000, I had these recordings, and through Ben, I made some connections to music industry people. I was the very definition of naive and had no idea what I was doing. I'd just been making music with no thought that people might want to hear it. I've always felt that I owe Ben a great debt, because he became such a champion for my music and shared it with people who would change my life. He was talking to Mike McGonigal, who had a zine called *Yeti* that came with a CD, and Mike put my song "Dead Man's Will" on one of his compilations. At the same time, Ben was talking to Sub Pop about his own band, and he put my stuff in their ear. McGonigal's CD came out around then, so they heard it from two places and thought, *Maybe there's something here*. So they called me.

It's impossible to overstate how crazy it felt to never have pursued a music career and then have a label like Sub Pop interested. I knew that I was lucky, but I don't think I understood how lucky at the time. It was just an incredible feeling to be doing this thing by yourself and working hard at it and then have this label— which I had so much respect for—reach out and validate it all. Then came the conversation where they said, "Well, if we're going to put this record out, you should probably put a band together." It was terrifying! I was very much a behind-the-camera person with no experience performing. I was scared to death.

But I definitely wanted to make the most of the opportunity, so I just called some friends. I called my sister, since I knew she could sing. I called a friend named Patrick McKinney from Tallahassee who had a band I really liked and had helped me work on some film scores. And my friend E.J. Holowicki, an old roommate in Tallahassee who helped me record my first stuff, he came along to play bass. All of a sudden, we were going on tour for the first time!

That's when Sub Pop was also putting out the Ugly Casanova record from Isaac Brock of Modest Mouse, so they asked him to take me on tour. He wanted to audition me first. Looking back, it sounds silly, but he wasn't wrong—I'd never played a show! So Jonathan and Megan from Sub Pop and Isaac all came to Miami, and I picked them up at the airport. I had a friend named Brook Dorsch who had an art gallery with a big yard in Wynwood, a neighborhood that's very different now but at the time was a dump. We put on a little party, a group of friends came, and we had a cookout and played a show among the folding chairs. An entertainer at heart, Isaac bought a euro-style banana-hammock bathing suit printed with an American flag, and he got up and played some songs, too. It all felt a bit like a dream, but it must have gone all right because I got the job.

About a Bruise

A weed believes the garden
Sunday clothes don't fool me
The sky is full of our prayer
When you were making moonlight
For mall cops in Mobile
The night fell from their eyes

This is borrowed stone
I'd help you let your hair down
Point to birds, then you'd say bang
The sun left every evening
Good grass was dying
You drew your dawn on the world

Tenderness to you was only talk about a bruise
Or walking into water after dark

Your papa saw me coming
Blood knows when it's worth it
All you said, you said like a song
Jesus left a best friend
Mine says forget her
His field is waiting for wind

Mobile had your moonlight
But that line cook had candy
You let it blow your candle a bit
Ring a bell that's broken
That sound is loud inside us
Flowing farther away

Tenderness to you is only talk about a bruise
Or walking into water after dark

Love can last a lifetime
This is Alabama
Any wheel is forgiving the road
Now you're making music
For beautiful people by the sea
Who don't need a song

All in Good Time

All in good time I gave it my best
I was alone until I found myself
Grew up to be a man more or less
All in good time

All in good time I drifted away
I ran my mouth 'til I'd nothing to say
You broke my heart then I was okay
All in good time

All in good time I trusted my eyes
Treated my losses
like clouds in the sky
Finally picked on someone my size
All in good time

All in good time I followed my nose
Learned where to bleed
when a night comes to blows
Tried on your love
then I folded those clothes
All in good time

Throw your bread to falling birds
Buried friends and wasted words
Something wants to eat us all alive

All in good time my angel came back
Made us some money
but that didn't last
We wouldn't cry but we couldn't laugh
All in good time

All in good time we fell like a star
We closed our eyes
and we opened our arms
Ran off the road in our own stolen car
All in good time

All in good time and that's what's it was
We mistook that cash in the
mattress for love
Dropped all our weapons
and shrank from the blood
All in good time

All in good time we'd nothing to prove
We took the bait until we lost a tooth
No one believed it but we told the truth
All in good time

All in good time our plan went to shit
I told my future by reading your lips
You wore my ring until it didn't fit
All in good time

All in good time we suffered enough
We met our muscle
when push came to shove
Swept all that broken glass
under the rug
All in good time

Dancing 'til we both collapse
Wishing we could hide our tracks
Something wants to eat us all alive

All in good time we'll remember when
Say our goodbyes and then hello again
Huff and we'll puff until they let us in
All in good time

All in good time we'll land on our feet
Your mother will sigh
and my soldier will sleep
We'll swim the ocean, fishes set free
All in good time

An Angry Blade

Who left you so?

Striking a match
for the keyhole
Dark as the
evening laid
When he left you
all alone

Turning to fade
through the sawgrass
Tall as the
only love
That you'll ever
really know

Who left you so?

Grace is a gift
for the fallen, dear
You're an angry blade
and you're brave
But you're
all alone

Turning a shade
of an angel born
In a bramble ditch
when the doors
Of heaven
closed

Angels Go Home

All our morning after sudden laughter
All our moons bloom overnight
Like our happy hour
plastic flowers
All our dreamers
lose to the light

Like our friendly fire, naked liars
And tired pomp and circumstance
All our true believers
break like fever
All our bruises
beg for a chance

All our sons and daughters
Throw their stones in holy water
All our angels
go home
All our friends and lovers
Take our clothes
and show their colors
All our angels
go home

Paper tigers, dumpster divers
All our phantoms
fixing their own hair
Our unforgiven
count their ammunition
All our mercy
leaves us unaware

All us sons and daughters
Throw our stones in holy water
All our angels
go home
All us friends and lovers
Take your clothes
and show our colors
All our angels
go home

Anyone's Game

Anybody born knows
how to play this little game
First they light a candle in themselves
They lean it up against the wind
and then they run around the rain
Anybody born plays pretty well

If they crawl into another's heart
while someone counts to ten
Let's just say
that's the hardest place to hide
They jump out of their names
until the game begins again
They open one another's empty eyes

Until they rise
like ashes off the ground
And fall down
like diamonds off the dead
Until they go as though they're coming back
And take their time like it's all they're gonna get

Anybody born knows
how to play this little game
No one can be born too many times
First they kiss their lucky dice
then they dig themselves a grave
They do this until its killing them to try

To rise
like ashes off the ground
And fall down
like diamonds off the dead
To go as though they're coming back
And take their time like it's all they're gonna get

Let's just say that the clues are few
and the last one in's an egg
They bend the map or just turn around
If their life gets in the way
Let's just say
That their life gets in the way

15

Arms of a Thief

Mr. Henry and the muscle man
Gave her shoes on a night there
was no room to stand
And like a letter in a stolen purse
She was bored of her weight,
she was bored of her words
The daughter of a soldier
told the fallen priest
"It's a cold, cold place in the arms of a thief"
And reaching out to touch the steering wheel
She said, "Leave me alone but
just don't leave me here, alright?"

Mr. Henry and another guy
Gave her gold on a night that
it fell from the sky
And like her body when the buzzard came
She was bored of her luck,
she was bored of her name
The daughter of a lawyer
told the fallen priest
"It's a cold, cold place in the arms of a thief"
And dabbing at the arrow in her heel
She said, "Leave me alone but
just don't leave me here, alright?"

Mr. Henry was a dying man
With advice in a tongue that
she didn't understand
And like the water when the sea got rough
She was bored of the breeze,
she was bored of her love
The winner and the loser
told the fallen priest
"It's a cold, cold place in the arms of a thief"
And holding everything he made her steal
She said, "Leave me alone but
just don't leave me here, alright?

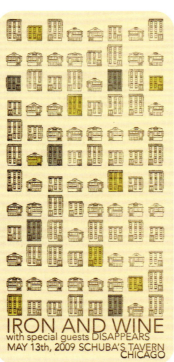
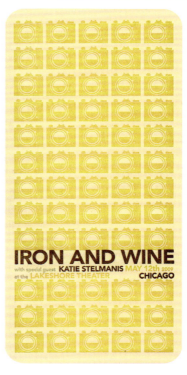
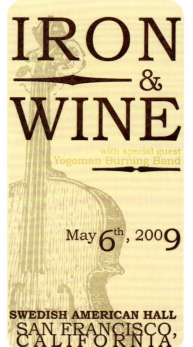

Autumn Town Leaves

In this autumn town where the leaves can fall
On either side of the garden wall
We laugh all night to keep the embers glowing
Some are leaping free from their moving cars
Stacking stones around their broken hearts
Waving down any wind that might come blowing

Mice move out when the field is cut
Serpents curl when the sun comes up
Songbirds only end up where they're going
Some get rain and some get snow
Some want love and some want gold
I just want to see you in the morning

Dogs lay down in the evening heat
Fish do worse when they leave the sea
Songbirds only end up where they're going

In this autumn town where the lights can change
Some get mercy and some get blame
Some get lost when they feel the river flowing
It's all holy smoke and the flame dies fast
We hold our hats while the days fly past
Cold wind comes and we wave but it keeps going

Fathers, sons, and holy ghosts
All come back or they all come close
Songbirds only end up where they're going
Some get hard and some go home
Some want flesh and some want bone
I just want to see you in the morning

Baby Center Stage

Mama called you "baby center stage"
She could really run her mouth
Baton Rouge called you "petite ange"
When Birmingham had run you out

Doesn't anybody see how scared you are?
There was a time I was running you down
But the world kept spinning round
Doesn't anybody see how scared you are?
There was a time when you were running to me
But the lightning spared the tall tree

When your moon lights up the riverside
Slinging mud and bad blood
You can call me anytime
For all its worth, Louisiana's still not enough

In your restless days
I got lost, I got saved
In your restless nights
I swung blind
Somehow falling into the light

Doesn't anybody see how scared you are?
There was a time I was running you down
But the world kept spinning round
Doesn't anybody see how scared you are?
There was a time when you were running to me
But the hurricane had mercy

In your restless days
All that wind, all those waves
In your restless nights
We closed our eyes
Killed each other and came to life
In your restless days
I made my bed, I dug my grave
In your restless nights
We both swung blind
Somehow falling into the light

Bag of Cats

There's a wealth of opportunity
clinging to the world
You'll never find a better place to die
Love walks down the street
With the kind of missing teeth
you laugh about

Look at all the loneliness
sneaking through our dreams
Little bugs that bang into the light
Love will find a way
At least that's what you say to kid around

Treat an opportunity like its treating you
Another plum thumbing for a ride
Love is only fair
Until all its favorite hair has fallen out

Let's laugh at ourselves
When we listen again
It'll blend with the sound of the rain
Let's paint with our blood
Draw some lines in the sand
If the wind isn't blowing our way
Let's say what's on our minds
Like we know how we feel
And just what we're feeling it for
Like life isn't outside the door
With its bag of cats

Think of all the beautiful people saying please
If you're gonna do something, do it right
Love is in the air
I couldn't tell you where but it's around

The wealth of opportunity
keeps clinging to the world
We've blown a million kisses in the sky
Love has no regrets
Or hasn't had one yet to talk about

Belated Promise Ring

Sunday morning,
my Rebecca's sleeping in with me again
There's a kid outside the church kicking a can
When the cedar branches twist,
she turns her collar to the wind
The weather can close the world
within its hand

And my mother says Rebecca is
as stubborn as they come
They both call to me with words I never knew
There's a bug inside the thimble,
there's a band-aid on her thumb
And a pony in the river turning blue
They say time may give you more than
your poor bones could ever take
My Rebecca says she never wants a boy
To be barefoot on the driveway
as they wave and ride away
Then to run inside and curse the open door

I once gave to my Rebecca
a belated promise ring
And she sold it to the waitress on a train
I may find her by the phone booth
with a fashion magazine
She may kiss me when her girlfriends leave again
They say time may give you more than
your poor bones could ever take
I think I could never love another girl
To be free atop a tree stump
and to look the other way
While she shines my mother's imitation pearls

Sunday evening,
my Rebecca's lost a book she never read
And the moon already fell into the sea
So the statues of our fathers in the courthouse flowerbed
Now they blend with all the lightning tattered trees
They say time may give you more than
your poor bones could ever take
My Rebecca said she knew I'd want a boy
A dollar for my boardwalk red balloon to float away
She would earn a pocketful to buy me more

Beneath the Balcony

Let's go out and dance, darling
Our last of days
And grace the game with a blindfold on
The cheaters came to play
And outside the soft-handed boys
Screaming cars and all their speed
Music, math, a hero begging change
His sword across his knees

And how he prays to find a man to blame
For every sleepless night he spends
And for every well that he warned me of
But wound up falling in
And then for the kids beneath the balcony
Who disregard the rain
To make sure the king won't grant
The dead man one more day

Let's go out and see, darling
What shines tonight
And temper your dream about the dying horse
With traffic, noise, and light
And somewhere the soft-handed boys
Bleeding hearts, and worker bees
Give to the holy mother begging change
Christ across her knees

And oh how she prays to find a man to blame
For every loveless night she waits
And for every gun that she frowned upon
But still some fucker made
And then for the kid beneath the balcony
Behind the garbage can
Who waits for the king to come
And hold his sweating hand

Beyond the Fence

Two flat tires on the Model T
Two birds fighting for a bug
Faded squares like snowy TV screens
Where your photographs were hung

Keep Old Glory folded on a shelf
In a cabinet full of guns
Sell that engine block to someone else
Maybe they can make it run

How'd that calf get out beyond the fence?
How'd that hole get in your jeans?
Movie show was once but twenty cents
That mud there was once a stream

The moon is high
Your nose is burned
Your dog is gone
Your mouth is dry
The milk has turned
But Barbara's home

Hand in hand you watch the sun go down
Colored lullaby of God
Barbara wears her mother's old night gown
Sleeping with the nightlight on

White sheet blowing on a short clothesline
New tree bending to the breeze
This clock's beautiful but can't keep time
What's that's scar on both your knees?

The moon is high
Your nose is burned
Your dog is gone
Your mouth is dry
The milk has turned
But Barbara's home

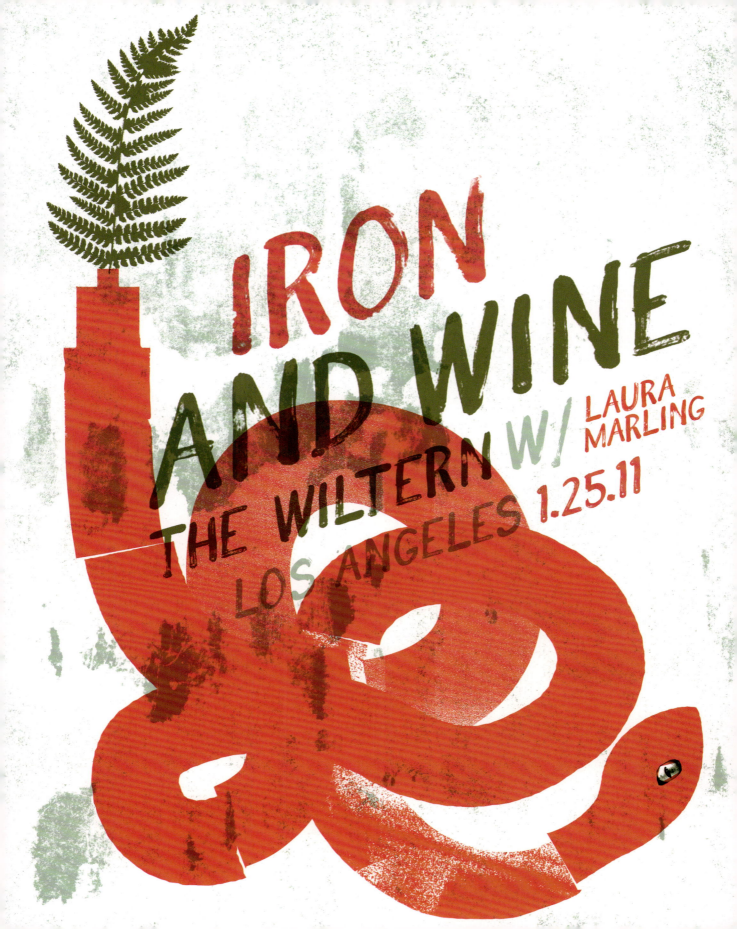

Big Burned Hand

When the arrogant goddess of love
came to steal my shoes
She had a white-hot pistol
and a homemade heart tattoo
Singing, "One's to give
and one's to take away
But neither of them
will keep you off your knees"
Her children bowed
and bolted off the stage
While the lion and the lamb kept
fighting for the shade tree

When the winsome god of war
came to set me free
He had a couple of coke bottles
full of gasoline
Singing, "All I love
is all that I allow"
And he blew me a kiss
off a big burned hand
I nearly choked
with smoke and fell down
While the lion and the lamb
kept shooting at a tin can

When the gun-shy goddess of love
came back to patch things up
She had a purple heart and
mother's milk in a plastic cup
Singing, "One will lay you
gently in the grave
And one's the flag you
fold before you go"
When the curtain rose
the crowd was blown away
While the lion and the lamb
kept fucking in the back row

Bird Stealing Bread

Tell me, baby, tell me
Are you still on the stoop
Watching the windows close?
I've not seen you lately
On the street by the beach
Or places we used to go

I've a picture of you
On our favorite day
By the seaside
There's a bird stealing bread
That I brought
Out from under my nose

Tell me, baby, tell me
Does his company make
Light of a rainy day
How I've missed you lately
And the way we would speak
And all that we wouldn't say

Do his hands in your hair
Feel a lot like a thing
You believe in
Or a bit like a bird stealing bread
Out from under your nose

Tell me, baby, tell me
Do you carry the words
Around like a key or change
I've been thinking lately
Of a night on the stoop
And all that we wouldn't say

If I see you again
On the street by the beach
In the evening
Will you fly like a bird stealing bread
Out from under my nose

Biting Your Tail

May your eyes be wide and seeing
May you learn from the view where you're kneeling
Know the fear of the world that you're feeling
Is the fear of a slave
May you know how the fight was started
And want as much from the snake as the garden
And wear them both like a glove that you can wave

May your mouth betray your wisdom
May you get what they fail to mention
May your love be your only religion
And preach it to us all
May you lose what you offer gladly
May you worship the time and its passing
The stars won't ever wait for you to watch them fall

We're the smoke on a burned horizon
We're the boat on a tide that's rising
Both the post and the pig you're untying
The butcher gone for the blade
Someday we may all be happy
Someday all make a face worth slapping
Someday we may be shocked to be laughing
At the way we behaved

May your hands be strong and willing
May you know when to speak and to listen
May you find every friend that you're missing
There's no check in the mail
May you end it bruised and purple
And know that peace is the shape of a circle
Cause round and round you'll go
Biting your tail

We're the children the wind is whipping
The short hands on a clock still ticking·
Both the egg and the red fox grinning
Its belly full for the day
Someday we may all want nothing
And all forget that we'll get what's coming
Someday all say, "The world was something
That we just couldn't change"

May your tongue be something wicked
And know your part in the calf and the killing
And see straight through the captain you're kissing
The helm loose in his hands
May your words be well worth stealing
And put your hand on your heart when you're singing
The choir's sick of the song but they've still got to stand

The Bitter Suite
(Pájaro / Evil Eye / Tennessee Train)

Este pájaro muerto quiere alas
pero no lo recuerda
Hay sueños lo suficientemente salvajes
para pasar el tiempo

My first mom laughed like she never had
She dug a heal deep into the mountainside
You know Grace who gave me back a golden ring
She always knew what was hers and what was mine

I was only stumbling
through her garden gate
Trains leave Tennessee moaning
as they roll away

My last dad was clean as he could ever be
Leaning through a window, rubbing at his evil eye
Last I heard he saw it all for what it was
There are dreams wild enough to pass the time

Then again, there's all we could
trade for a hiding place
Trains leave Tennessee moaning
as they roll away

This dead bird wants the wings he can't recall
A weak preacher standing with a song to sing
Who knows grace staring at a kitchen fire
That's the way I told her I would give her anything

Anything wasn't enough
to make her stay
Trains leave Tennessee moaning
as they roll away

Bitter Truth

Our missing pieces walked between us
When we were moving through the door
You called them mine
I called them yours

You would make me get so angry
But then I'd stay there on my own
We've both made peace
But all alone

Some call it talking blues
Some call it bitter truth
Some call it getting even in a song

I kept reading hidden meanings
You would rage how I was wrong
That life was too short
And you'd stayed too long

Let's be honest, we were strongest
Until I let you drag me down
If I was sorry then
I'm not now

Some get a garden heart
Some get a riverside
Some get a house that lets the years go by

That life has ended, you seem contented
While the graveside flowers die
I call them yours
You call them mine

Nothing makes silence like experience
There's a message in my eyes
You better love yourself
'Cause I've tried

Some call it talking blues
Some call it bitter truth
Some call it getting even in a song

Black Candle

I counted my luck
and I went with my brother
To where the witch on the hill
threw the bones of her mother
To where the bravest birds
in the height of the sky
Tumble down the mountainside
And gather to pray
like a blanket on the fallen pines
Like praying ain't
a waste of time

She told me again
that she knew I'd be coming
While she padded her gown
with all my counterfeit money
And said, "Your love is locked
in the garden you've grown
Like a soldier's wound
that bleeds through his clothes
So pick up your gun and pray
there's no one left to fight
Like praying ain't
a waste of time"

I said, "You've given me less
than you know I can handle"
So the witch on the hill
lit a single black candle
And said, "The name of god is carved on a blade
The wheels you make
will turn in flame
So pray
for love and the world to pray in kind
Like praying ain't
a waste of time"

Boy with a Coin

A boy with a coin
he found in the weeds
With bullets and pages
of trade magazines
Close to a car
that flipped on the turn
When God left the ground
to circle the world

A girl with a bird
she found in the snow
Then flew up her gown
and that's how she knows
That God made her eyes
for crying at birth
Then left the ground
to circle the Earth

A boy with a coin
he crammed in his jeans
Then, making a wish,
he tossed in the sea
Walked to a town
that all of us burned
When God left the ground
to circle the world

BOY WITH A COIN
E FOUND IN THE WEEDS
ITH BULLETS AND BONES
AT WASHED OFF THE STREET
E SLEPT IN SOME TOWN
HE PEOPLE HAD BURNED
HEN GOD LEFT THE GROUND
~~TO~~ CIRCLE THE WORLD

A GIRL WITH A BIRD
HE FOUND IN THE SNOW
T FLEW UP HER GOWN

ATS ~~WHEN~~ NOW SHE KNOWS
AT GOD MADE HER EYES
R CRYING AT BIRTH
D THEN LEFT THE GROUND
 CIRCLE THE EARTH

BOY WITH A COIN
E ~~FOUND~~ IN HIS JEANS
HISPERED A WISH
ND TOSSED IN THE SEA
EN ~~ROSE FROM~~ THE CAR
E FLIPPED ON THE TURN
HEN GOD LEFT THE GROUND
O CIRCLE THE WORLD

Burn That Broken Bed

How do you bust the clouds
Grass on your back and hanging in the air
I want to scope you out
I wanna touch your mouth when you're up there

When are you coming back
Bird on a branch will come back home to sing
When are you coming back
Bringing it back and singing what you bring

How do you bust the clouds
Head on the ground and feeling what you see
I want to scope you out
I want to be your eyes and show you me

When are you coming back
When are you going to burn that broken bed
When are you coming back
I want to see you drifting overhead

Call It Dreaming

Say it's here where our pieces fall in place
Any rain softly kisses us on the face
Any wind means we're running
We can sleep and see them coming
Where we drift and call it dreaming
We can weep and call it singing

Where we break when our hearts are strong enough
We can bow because our music's warmer than blood
Where we see enough to follow
We can hear when we are hollow
Where we keep the light we're given
We can lose and call it living

Where the sun isn't only sinking fast
Every night knows how long it's supposed to last
Where the time of our lives is all we have
And we get a chance to say before we ease away
For all the love you've left behind, you can have mine

Say it's here where our pieces fall in place
We can fear because a feelings fine to betray
Where our water isn't hidden
We can burn and be forgiven
Where our hands hurt from healing
We can laugh without a reason

Because the sun isn't only sinking fast
Every moon and our bodies make shining glass
Where the time of our lives is all we have
And we get a chance to say before we ease away
For all the love you've left behind, you can have mine

WHERE THE SUN ONLY FALLS INTO YOUR
EVERY NIGHT KNOWS HOW LONG ITS SUPPOSE
WHERE ~~THE~~ THE TIME OF OUR LIVES IS
AND WE GET A CHANCE TO SAY
~~WHERE EVERY NIGHT WE SAY~~
BEFORE WE ~~DRIFT~~ EASE AWAY
(IF THERE'S ANY) FOR ALL THE LOVE YOU'VE LEFT BEHIN
YOU CAN HAVE MINE

CAUSE THE MOON ISN'T HIDING IN THE GRASS

EVERY MOON AND OUR BODIES MAKE SHINING G

CALL IT DREAMING

SAY ITS HERE WHERE OUR PIECES FALL IN PLACE
ANY RAIN SOFTLY KISSES US ON THE FACE
~~WHERE THE~~ ANY WIND MEANS WERE RUNNING
WE CAN SLEEP AND SEE THEM COMING
WHERE WE DRIFT AND CALL IT DREAMING
WE CAN WEEP AND CALL IT SINGING

WHERE WE BREAK WHEN OUR HEARTS ARE STRONG ENOUGH
WE CAN BOW CAUSE OUR MUSIC'S WARMER THAN BLOOD
WHERE WE SEE ENOUGH TO FOLLOW
WE CAN HEAR WHEN WE ARE HOLLOW
WHERE WE KEEP THE LIGHT WE'RE GIVEN
WE CAN LOSE AND CALL IT LIVING

SAY ITS HERE WHERE OUR PIECES FALL IN PLACE
WE CAN FEAR CAUSE A FEELING'S FINE TO BETRAY
WHERE OUR WATER ISN'T HIDDEN
WE CAN BURN AND BE FORGIVEN
WHERE OUR HANDS HURT FROM HEALING
WE CAN LAUGH WITHOUT A REASON
~~CAUSE THE SUN ONLY FALLS INTO YOUR LAP~~
CAUSE THE SUN ISN'T ONLY SINKING FAST
EVERY NIGHT KNOWS HOW LONG ITS SUPPOSED TO LAST
WHERE THE TIME OF OUR LIVES IS ALL WE HAVE
AND WE GET A CHANCE TO SAY
BEFORE WE EASE AWAY
"FOR ALL THE LOVE YOU'VE LEFT BEHIND,"
"YOU CAN HAVE MINE"

Call Your Boys

Call your boys now that the table's set and shining
No one's seen any of them in many days
Call your boys, they shot a buzzard off the Chrysler
And you still taste all that you swallowed before grace

And you'll forgive even the time they burned the henhouse
And ran from you, ran to the hills with burning hands

Setting sun framed in the doorway right behind you
Several chores, surely some lessons left to tell
Setting sun, wolves in the hills and now before you
Sit your boys, each with his shining silverware

They'll bury you under the wood beside the carport
Bury you, some neon stop along the way

Radio fuzz on the fencepost by the pasture
Long ago, Liza and you would dance all day
Now you lay buried, the stern and sacred father
In sacred earth under a billboard in the rain

One last toast, here's to the brave who went before us
Who died in vain, died in a movie for a dream

Calm on the Valley

There's a rooster, a hen,
a black dog by my kid in the yard
And I've tattooed the head
of the woman I've wed on my arm
We sit on the lawn and she
winks as she yawns at the sound
That the setting sun makes as it
lights up the lake and goes down

And you ease my troubles
with your hands
Like the night puts
a calm on the valley
Moved my shaking castle
from the sand
When you gave me your soul
for to marry

The cicadas in tune ain't too
noisy for you or too fast
As the night eases in,
a dark wine on our skin and the grass
Now the moon's high above,
you're the woman I've loved for so long
It's the last goodnight kiss and these
moments I miss when you're gone

And you ease my troubles
with your hand
Like the night puts a calm
on the valley
Moved my shaking
castle from the sand
When you gave me your soul
for to marry

Carousel

Almost home
When I missed the bottom stair
You were braiding your gray hair
It had grown so long
Since I'd been gone

And the perfect girls
By the pool, they would protest
The cross around their necks
But our sons were overseas
And we all know about
the hive and the honeybees

Almost home
With an olive branch and a dove
You were beating on a Persian rug
With your Bible and your wedding band
Both hidden on the TV stand

When a cruel wind blew
Every city father fell
Off the county carousel
While the dogs were eating snow
All our sons had sunk
in a trunk of Noah's clothes

Almost home
And got lost on our new street
While your grieving girls all died in their sleep
So the dogs all went unfed
A great dream of bones
all piled on the bed

And the cops couldn't care
When that crackhead built a boat
And said, "Please, before I go
May our only honored bond
Be the kinship of the kids
in the riot squad"

Carried Home

The kettle burned
because I left it too long
When we were kissing
with the radio on
The cat was choking
on a rattlesnake bone
The town had gathered around
the soldier boy carried home

The sick kids ate
a bowl of red clay
And every summer day
was ending in rain
The late judge teetered
in a jon boat
The town had gathered around
the soldier boy carried home

The broken window
and the pretty blue sky
And cold water for my
swollen black eye
We shook some money
from your mother's old clothes
When all had gathered around
the soldier boy carried home

Caught in the Briars

The back alley's full of rain
And everything's shining
As holy as she can be
The trick's in the timing
Free as the morning birds
Fragile as china
She's stuck in the weakest heart
Of South Carolina
Where all of the naked boys
Who lay down beside her
Sing her the saddest song
All caught in the briars

I never meant to fall
So hard in her doorway
All of the sinners here
Have crosses for Sunday
Kissed at the county fair
Frisked in the city
Where proof is an answered prayer
But ain't it a pity
That all of the naked boys
Who lay down beside her
Sing her the saddest song
All caught in the briars

Our Endless Numbered Days

If *The Creek Drank the Cradle* was born out of living alone, *Our Endless Numbered Days* was very much painted by domestic life.

Kim and I had met years earlier, in art school in Richmond, then we'd split up for a while. By 2001 she had a daughter, Ruth, and was thinking about studying midwifery at a birthing center in Miami. I said, "Come stay with me while you check out the school," and one thing led to another.

They moved in, and I became an immediate dad. Ruth was three. Kim and I got married in the summer of 2002, literally a month after we went on that first tour. And my first daughter was born a month after that. Busy times! My place was too small, so we moved to a different apartment in north Miami Beach. And for the next several years, I was so busy with kids and work that I really had to carve out writing time. I would take the kids to school, come home, and those next three hours were mine, before I had to go do a bunch of chores or teach a class. The writing never felt like a chore to me. It was just the first time I'd ever had to be disciplined about it.

The new themes in these songs were because my life had changed. I don't really write diary songs, but you're definitely using the bolt of cloth that you have from your experience as a launching place for your fiction. We were starting a family, the exciting part where you look out and all you see is horizon line. And being a dad teaches you a lot about yourself! I had a new emotional experience, a new perspective, and I was starting to think about things differently than before.

Also, I had a band now! That meant I could do different kinds of songs. The style wasn't terribly different—it was only a year later, so I was still working from the same palette—but I didn't know what the Iron & Wine thing would be. I was curious. I was looking for a new way to communicate, whether it was through the band, or different chords, or more open tunings on the guitar.

I was adamant about going into the studio to make this album. And on the Ugly Casanova tour, I had met Brian Deck. He was the drummer and had produced that record. His bands Red Red Meat and Califone were a big deal for me, so to get to hang out with him was really exciting, an inspiration. Percussion was something I was eager to experiment with, something I didn't really have access to with the home-recorded stuff. So I started talking to Brian about recording the next record.

We went up to Chicago, to Engine Studios, and stayed in a little apartment there. Smoked a lot of cigarettes. In hindsight it seems silly, but we still basically recorded the same way I had done it at home—record one track, then another, overdubbing and then overdubbing some more. There was no live performance of the band playing together. I wasn't ready to grow out of my habit of carefully polishing what I was making. It seems so tedious. It's crazy! But Brian was really patient.

I remember being frustrated a bit at first by the cleaner sound and wondering if I was doing the right thing. I'd become very accustomed to my approach at home, and now the sound was so different. It felt unfamiliar. But I was happy to keep trying different things. I was learning a lot about mics, about mixing on a real board and everything. I remember feeling really unmoored, which I can look back at now and see was good. Being out of your comfort zone is hard while you're in it, but it's an opportunity to evolve. When I hear it now, it's easy to pick stuff out that I could change, but I think it's a really fun portrait of where I was at the time.

In all honesty, performing these songs now can sometimes feel a bit like reciting the Pledge of Allegiance. You end up playing them so many times that it becomes difficult to really engage with them emotionally. But not always. They're very tender songs, very unguarded and vulnerable. To perform them in front of a big group of people who are celebrating and recognizing and valuing that is really powerful. It's one thing to get up and rock out. That's super fun. But there's something unique and special about getting together and celebrating frailty.

Cinder and Smoke

Give me your hand
The dog in the garden row is covered in mud
And dragging your mother's clothes
Cinder and smoke
The snake in the basement
Found the juniper shade
The farmhouse is burning down

Give me your hand
And take what you will tonight, I'll give it as fast
And high as the flame will rise
Cinder and smoke
Some whispers around the trees
The juniper bends
As if you were listening

Give me your hand
Your mother is drunk as all the firemen shake
A photo from father's arms
Cinder and smoke
You'll ask me to pray for rain
With ash in your mouth
You'll ask it to burn again

Claim Your Ghost

Our winter keeps running us down
We wake up with love hanging on
Our killers let go
Killers let go

Some kids get a handful of rain
Our hope is the desperate die wise
Our killers let go
Killers let go

Morning falls from a tree
And asks for a name
Claim your ghost
Know the wine for what it is

The garden grows into our street
We're holding the blossoms up high
Our killers let go
Killers let go

Claim your ghost
Know the wine for what it is

There's light holding onto the ground
Our music is clumsy and free
Our killers let go
Killers let go

Cold Town

Magazines and paperbacks
The perfect rainy day
Jenny's packed the car by now
And probably on her way

Rise and put the kettle on
This feeling calls for tea
Tommy get the telephone
It wouldn't be for me

Spring feels so far away
When you're unforgiven
Now that Jenny's away
It's a cold town to live in

Evening brings a break in rain
The dog goes back outside
Thomas says that I should sleep
Just to pass the time

Close the door and cross the room
The moonlight wanders in
Crawl in bed with her perfume
The rain begins again

Spring feels so far away
When you're unforgiven
Now that Jenny's away
It's a cold town to live in

Communion Cups and Someone's Coat

Talk of yesterday
and she will show her
Brothers photographed
in callous clothes
Say tomorrow
and she'll say, "Come find me
On a beach and
there will be no moon"
But say today
And she will kiss your face
And maybe forget

Talk of yesterday
like bargain shoe string
She will kick the car
and find her friends
Say tomorrow
and then she'll describe some
Old communion cups
and someone's coat
But say today
and she may look your way
And lead you home

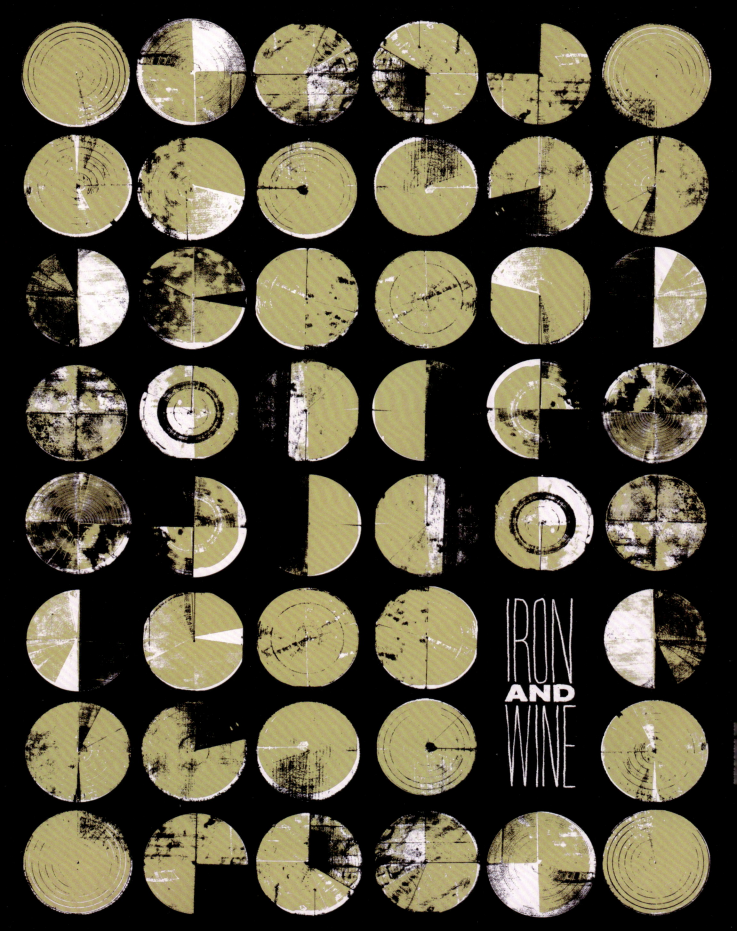

LIGHT VERSE — IRON AND WINE

JUNE 14 MILWAUKEE, WI 15 ST. PAUL, MN 17 DENVER, CO 18 SALT LAKE CITY, UT 20 SEATTLE, WA 21 PORTLAND, OR 22 PORTLAND, OR 23 VANCOUVER, BC 25 OAKLAND, CA 27 MONTEREY, CA 28 LOS ANGELES, CA 29 LOS ANGELES, CA 30 EL CAJON, CA JULY 2 PHOENIX, AZ 3 TAOS, NM 5 TULSA, OK 6 ST. LOUIS, MO 8 CHICAGO, IL 31 NEW ORLEANS, LA AUGUST 1 HOUSTON, TX 2 AUSTIN, TX 3 DALLAS, TX 5 ATLANTA, GA 6 WILMINGTON, NC 7 RALEIGH, NC 9 WASHINGTON, DC 10 PHILADELPHIA, PA 11 BOSTON, MA 13 NEW HAVEN, CT 14 BROOKLYN, NY 16 MONTREAL, QC 17 TORONTO, ON 18 DETROIT, MI 20 CLEVELAND, OH 22 INDIANAPOLIS, IN 23 LOUISVILLE, KY 24 NASHVILLE, TN OCTOBER 22 BELFAST, IRELAND 23 DUBLIN, IRELAND 25 EDINBURGH, UK 26 MANCHESTER, UK 27 BRISTOL, UK 29 BIRMINGHAM, UK 30 LONDON, UK 31 CAMBRIDGE, UK NOVEMBER 2 GRONINGEN, NETHERLANDS 4 COPENHAGEN, DENMARK 5 STOCKHOLM, SWEDEN 6 OSLO, NORWAY 7 GOTENBURG, SWEDEN 9 HAMBURG, GERMANY 11 BERLIN, GERMANY 12 COLOGNE, GERMANY 14 AMSTERDAM, NETHERLANDS 15 ANTWERP, BELGIUM 2024

Cutting It Close

Long lost friend of mine
I know we only fucked a couple of times
Love owes nothing to us
Nobody's perfect or as dumb as their luck
Kissing this, kissing that
I'm kissing anybody kissing me back
Time likes pulling my teeth
I never knew how many teeth I would need
So it goes and it goes
It doesn't matter but its cutting it close

Anyway, life is long
Could be a little longer don't get me wrong
And its lights won't leave me alone
Crooked fingers keep pointing me home
Going here, going there
I'm leaving heaven but I couldn't say where
Love keeps ringing a bell
Clear water for the well in myself
Or just a hand for the glove
It doesn't matter 'til it totally does

Miracles never cease
Depending on which ones you believe
I've stopped holding my breath
People are passing out hoping for less
Anyway, how you been
Look at everybody twist in the wind
Time just does what it does
I only wish it wouldn't do it to us

Dead Man's Will

Give this stone to my brother
Because we found it playing in the barnyard
Many years ago

Give this bone to my father
He'll remember hunting in the hills
When I was ten years old

May my love reach you all
I locked it in myself and buried it too long
Now that I've come to fall
Please say it's not too late
Now that I'm dead and gone

Give this string to my mother
It pulled the baby teeth she keeps
Inside the drawer

Give this ring to my lover
I was scared and stupid not to ask
For her hand long before

May my love reach you all
I locked it in myself and buried it too long
now that I've come to fall
Please say it's not too late
Now that I'm dead and gone

Dearest Forsaken

To my dearest forsaken
Who the earth now has taken
Empty, the bottle drains no more
It is true that I loved you
Despite the harm now on you
Wash us, the river has you boy

Here on the eve of too long
Where you'll think I have done wrong
Waking in fear of you no more
I put my trust in the Savior
The fuming forces of nature
The strength of the stump I tied you, boy

To my dearest forsaken
Dearest vow I have broken
Prey of your angry hand no more
I'll put my trust in the Savior
The river may have me later
Sleep with my lost love for you boy

The Desert Babbler

Its New Year's Eve
and California's gonna kill you soon
The Barstow boys,
buckeyes in the shadow of the moon
Black houses
in the hills and roadside hearts
Dying for a place
to fall apart
Who knew what you
could learn to live without
Mother Mary's
lying in your mouth
Back home the kitchen's
warm with Christmas wine
And every girl
has got an axe to grind
You left to look for heaven
But you're far
from that hard light tonight

So quietly we've
lost another year
The desert put
a babbler in your ear
Mean fireweed and
I miss you again
Barstow boys
are spit into the wind
Back home
the hammer always has to fall
Crosses barely
hanging on the wall
Someday I know
you'll never leave me
But we're far from
that hard light tonight

It's New Year's Eve
California's gonna kill you soon
The Barstow Boys
Buckeyes in the shadow of the moon
Black houses in the hills and roadside
Dying for a place to fall apart
Who knew what you could learn to live with. ort
Mother Mary's lying in your mouth
Back home the kitchen's warm with Christmas wine
And every girl has got an axe to grind
You left to look for heaven but we're far
From that hard light tonight
So ~~to feel another year~~
~~for~~ Quietly we've lost another year
The desert put a babbler in your far
Mean fireweed and I miss you again
Barstow boys are spit into the wind
Back home the hammer always has to fall
~~crosses~~ is barely hanging on the wall
Crosses I know you'll never leave me
Someday ~~I'll have to say goodbye~~ but we're far
From that hard light tonight

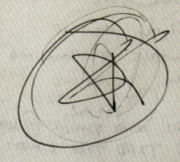

THE DESERT BABBLER

The Devil Never Sleeps

Dreaming again of a train track
ending at the edge of the sea
Big black cloud was
low and rolling our way
Dog at the barbed wire
barking at my buzz cut friends and me
Sound of a switchblade
shining in the summer rain
No one on the corner
had a quarter for the telephone
Everybody bitching,
"There's nothing on the radio"

Dreaming again of a city full of fathers
in their army clothes
Chattering boys and a chicken
at the chopping block
All of us lost at the crosswalk
waiting for the other to go
Didn't find a friend but,
boy, I really bought a lot
Someone bet a dollar that
my daddy wasn't coming home
Everybody bitching,
"There's nothing on the radio"

Dreaming again that it's freezing
and my mother's in her flowerbed
Long dead rows of daffodils and marigolds
Changing her face like a shadow on the gravel,
this is what she said
Blood on my chin still chewing on a red rose
"No one lives forever
and the devil never sleeps alone"
Everybody bitching,
"There's nothing on the radio"

Dirty Dream

Charleston begs for broken glass
And the morning clouds are blue
This little house is hardly ours
But I keep that bit from you
Time will take your breath away
And the shade from under the tree
But the quiet moon is close and now
You just woke up from a dirty dream

The harbor boats go back and forth
And the eyes come on at night
Someone stole your baby clothes
But I've tried to treat you right
Time will grind our bodies down
And the mountains into the sea
But the kid's asleep and you just woke up
From a dirty dream about you and me

Each Coming Night

Will you say when I'm gone away
"My lover came to me and we'd lay
In rooms unfamiliar but until now"

Will you say to them when I'm gone
"I loved your son for his sturdy arms
We both learned to cradle then live without"

Will you say when I'm gone away
"Your father's body was judgement day
We both dove and rose to the riverside"

Will you say to me when I'm gone
"Your face has faded but lingers on
Because light strikes a deal
with each coming night"

Eden

Whisper in my ear
Everything my dear
Every wicked vision that you carry
On your naked breast
I believe that was your best
Apple pie invention since we married

As God will be my judge
I'm not the man I was
Before I found you lying in the garden
Let's go buy some clothes
Some wool socks for your toes
'Cause it might be much colder in the morning

Elizabeth

Won't you sit down for a while?
I've been admiring your smile
How your eyes curl when you grin
Over your tonic and gin

Woman, we're harder than the frozen ground
When we don't trust a soul
Soft enough to have a crush
When we give up control
Elizabeth, do you see me tonight?

I'll be the first to admit
That I spend my time trying to fit
In circles too cold for my heart
Babe, can you tear that apart?

Woman, we're harder than the frozen ground
When we don't trust a soul
Soft enough to have a crush
When we give up control
Elizabeth, do you see me tonight?

Woman King

The records from around this time feel like one long developmental process. With *Our Endless Numbered Days*, I got my footing in the studio. So after that, it was time to keep pushing the sounds I could make. I wanted to incorporate more distortion, fuzz pedals—that seemed exciting. And I had two or three songs left over from *Our Endless Numbered Days* that we didn't use, so I thought I'd do a couple more and make an EP.

I like to set deadlines for myself, otherwise I keep tweaking things forever. So I'd set a random but aggressive due date to get back into the studio, then didn't really put the time in that I should have. At the end, I was cramming to finish these songs.

It was summer. We were at my in-laws' house in Virginia, on the Chesapeake Bay. I sequestered myself. Everyone else was on the beach playing, and I was holed up in an upstairs room with a guitar. I was working on some lyric ideas that ended up being a song called "Woman King," and in the room was a display case where my mother-in-law had a bunch of thimbles. They looked to me like little crowns. It sounds silly, but for some reason that association was enough to point me toward a group of songs. I put those very thimbles in their display case on the record cover.

I'd been playing with a bunch of biblical characters—Jezebel, Mary, Herod, Samson. The names are more a representation of an idea than a real person, but the similarity put a bow on a bunch of songs that weren't necessarily connected. Somehow, under the *Woman King* umbrella, they all felt of a piece.

We went back to Engine with the same personnel—same studio, same band—picking up the pieces from the last full-length, pushing the palette a little further, fleshing it out. The pedals and distortion brought out the aggression in some of the lyrics. The sleepy punk rocker in me loved it.

Evening on the Ground
(Lilith's Song)

Hey man
Evening on the ground
And there is no one else around
So you will
Blame me

Blame me for the rocks and baby bones
The broken lock on our garden

Garden wall of Eden
Full of spider bites and all your lovers
We were

We were born to fuck each other
One way or another

But I'll only lie
Down by the waterside at night

Hey man
Tiny baby tears
I will collect a million years
And you can blame me

Blame me, I will wear it
In the empty hollow part of my garden

Garden wall of Eden in the clamor
As they raise the curtain
You will

You will never make me
Learn to lay beneath the mountain

Because I'll only lie
Down by the waterside at night

Everyone's Summer of '95

Favorite cars sputter way too soon
Me and the boys from the billiards room
Found a shady tree, halfway home and going nowhere
Casey was asked for his favorite joke
It fluttered away just before he spoke
But it came to me, halfway home and going nowhere

All I can tell you is how we spent the time
Friends are made in the strangest ways
And I miss them by and by

Late in the day and the dust kicked up
Me and the boys with the windows shut
And the music on, halfway home and going nowhere
Everyone's summer of '95
Vivid and there 'til the tape head died
On our favorite song, halfway home and going nowhere

Hitching a ride with a crusty girl
Me and the boys stole a tie dye shirt
And a kiss or two, halfway home and going nowhere
Casey was wise with the mud flap guy
Smothered and bruised in the neon light
And we all went down, halfway home and going nowhere

All I can tell you is how we spent the time
Friends are made in the strangest ways
And I'll miss them by and by

Back on our feet and the car back soon
Me and the boys at the billiards room
Coming back on beer, halfway home and going nowhere
Casey will crack how the fight broke loose
I'm in the back thinking I must choose
But I like it here, halfway home and going nowhere

Ex-Lover Lucy Jones

This is the place where I met my Lucy Jones
I marked it well with a sacred stack of stones
I'll be here when she comes back in town
From overseas where she's been traveling 'round

A letter came from my sweetheart Lucy Jones
She said she's fine but I shouldn't try to phone
Her anymore, 'cause calling costs too much
And ended there, concise and quite abrupt

Have you heard from my ex-lover Lucy Jones
Who crossed the sea and left me here all alone
With naught to do but whittle on a bone
And sit upon a heavy stack of stones?

Faded from the Winter

Daddy's ghost behind you
Sleeping dog beside you
You're a poem of mystery
You're the prayer inside me

Spoken words like moonlight
You're the voice that I like

Needlework and seedlings
In the way you're walking
To me from the timbers
Faded from the winter

Father Mountain

While my father built a
mansion on the mountain
I was chasing my Teresa around a tree
We were kicking precious stones
Sinking ships and swimming home
Only crazy for the
comfort of our clothes

While my father built a
mansion on the mountain
My Teresa dragged a rag across my brow
She said, "The weather's only fair
The wind can only blow your hair"
And I believed her well enough
or didn't care

Everyone knows
and they don't know
Chandelier light
ain't love
It just watches
the time go
Across the marble floor
Out the ornamental door
Even rain can hear it
running off the road

While my father built a
mansion on the mountain
My Teresa threw me kisses through the cold
We read the writing on the wall
Braced each other for the fall
There's only one way
off a mountain after all

While my father built a
mansion on the mountain
It was me and my Teresa against the world
We took all the river had to give
Broke a bed and bought a crib
And left the mountain mansion
nothing to forgive

Fever Dream

Some days her
shape in the doorway
Will speak to me
A bird's wing on the window
Sometimes I'll hear
when she's sleeping
Her fever dream
A language on her face

"I want your flowers
like babies want god's love
Or maybe as sure as
tomorrow will come"

Some days,
like rain on the doorstep
She'll cover me
With grace in all she offers
Sometimes I'd like just to ask her
What honest words
She can't afford to say, like

"I want your flowers
like babies want god's love
Or maybe as sure as
tomorrow will come"

Flightless Bird, American Mouth

I was a quick wet boy
diving too deep for coins
All of your streetlight eyes
wide on my plastic toys
Then when the cops closed the fair,
I cut my long baby hair
Stole me a dog-eared map
and called for you everywhere

Have I found you,
flightless bird,
jealous, weeping
Or lost you,
American mouth
Big pill looming

Now I'm a fat house cat
nursing my sore blunt tongue
Watching the warm poison rats curl
through the wide fence cracks
Pissing on magazine photos,
those fishing lures
Thrown in the cold and clean
Blood of Christ mountain stream

Have I found you,
flightless bird,
grounded, bleeding
Or lost you,
American mouth
Big pill stuck going down

I WAS A QUICK WET BOY
DIVING ~~TOO~~ TOO DEEP FOR ~~CANDY~~ COINS
       FOR
ALL OF YOUR STREET LIGHT EYES
WIDE ON MY PLASTIC TOYS
THEN WHEN THE COPS CLOSED THE FAIR
            LONG
I CUT MY ∧ BABY HAIR
STOLE ME A ~~PICTURE BIKE~~ DOG-EARED MAP
~~CALLED~~ CALLING OUT
~~LOOKED FOR YOU~~ EVERYWHERE

HAVE
~~I~~ I FOUND YOU, FLIGHTLESS BIRD
~~SCARED OF SINGING~~ ?
JEALOUS, WEEPING?
OR LOST YOU, AMERICAN MOUTH,
                            LOOMING
BIG PILL STUCK / GOING DOWN?"

NOW I'M A FAT HOUSE CAT
NURSING MY SORE BLUNT TONGUE
WATCHING THE WARM POISONED RATS
CURL
~~QUEEZE~~ THROUGH THE WIDE FENCE CRACKS

PISSING ON MAGAZINE~~S~~
PHOTOS LIKE FISHING LURES
~~MAGAZINE~~

THROWN IN A COLD AND CLEAN
BLOOD OF CHRIST MOUNTAIN STREAM
HAVE I FOUND YOU, FLIGHTLESS BIRD,
GROUNDED, BLEEDING?
    LOST YOU...

Follow the Water

I'll always say I love you still
All of that water ran down the hill
Every broken thing washes away

You saw my scars and called them skin
I saw your garden and gave it sin
Every savior needs someone to save

Two kids climbed on a roller coaster car
Got rattled on the track
Up and down, around and back
Whoever they were
No matter who they are
No one's walking off the same

When I fell out of the palm of your hand
with summer flowers
I followed the water
and found these friends of mine
Where small town thugs and lighting bugs
shine in their final hours
And their hearts all come out of
the cold in the nick of time

Some get lost in a storm
Others behind an old chest of drawers
Our field got swallowed in fog
Flowers and all

Everybody climbs on a roller coaster car
Rattled by the track
Up and down, around and back
Whoever I was
No matter who you are
No one's walking off the same

When I fell out of the palm of your hand
with summer flowers
I followed the water
and found these friends of mine
Where small town thugs and lightning bugs
shine in their final hours
And their hearts all come out of
the cold in the nick of time

Freckled Girl

Someday soon I'll just live over yonder
Bring you coffee to taste
Crossword puzzles to ponder

And I hope you're well
And you know that I love you
Though I write so seldom
And call every blue moon

There's some tall Georgia boy
Searching out a freckled girl with style
Wait 'til tomorrow

Someday soon when we hail from Atlanta
We won't need some Christmas
To spend time together

And I hope you're well
And you sleep every evening
Never lying awake
For your dreaming of children

There's some tall Georgia boy
Searching out a freckled girl with style
Wait 'til tomorrow

Free Until They Cut Me Down

When the men take me to the devil tree
I will be free and shining like before
Papa don't tell me what I should've done
She's the one who begged me
"Take me home"

When the wind wraps me like the reaper's hand
I will swing free until they cut me down
Papa don't tell me what I could've done
She's the one who begged me
"Take me home"

When the sea takes me like my mother's arms
I will breathe free as any word of god
Papa don't tell me what you would've done
She's the one who begged me
"Take me home"

Freedom Hangs Like Heaven

Mary, carry your babe
Bound up tight like lips around a whimper
Your fingers over my face
Blind eyed Sampson driven to the temple
And night birds digging until dawn
Freedom hangs like Heaven over everyone
Ain't nobody knows what the newborn holds
But his mama says he'll walk on water
And wander back home

Mary, carry your shame
Well past all those eyes across the avenue
Fish heads running from rain
You know I'll do anything you want me to
Lamp oil lovers may say
"Freedom hangs like Heaven over everyone"
Ain't nobody knows what the newborn holds
But his papa's going to hide shaking gristle
And shaking like bone

Mary, carry my name
Hoof marks hacked up all I had to offer you
Looked all over this place
Lost your portrait lately when the winter blew
In like Herod and them
Freedom hangs like Heaven over everyone
Anybody knows what the newborn holds
But a dollar says he'll lick that devil
And do it alone

Friends They Are Jewels

Dreamless sleep will fall
Like a deep poisoned well
On the steeple birds
And the red light hotel

So lay your pistol down, granny
The company men never came for you
But don't unknit your brow, granny
The mice in the yard
Ate the potted plants you grew

Pour your bitter tea
For our sweet liquored host
Perfect polished stones
But this breeze beats you both

So lay your pistol down, granny
The duty of men never fell to you
When you unknit your brow, granny
Your friends, they are jewels
Twice as beautiful and few

Glad Man Singing

Yonder come a glad man singing a song
About a soldier want a boot and a fallen angel
Naked as a fish at night
About a sad man climbed up a willow bough
And the cops are on the fence around the dog in the manger
And the mouth of the river is wide

Yonder come a glad man singing a song
About the bushes by the gas pump gone to flower
And a constant star collides
About a sad man saying, "They've forgotten how"
And a baby quit sucking when the milk went sour
And the mouth of the river is wide

About a sad man lost in the hammock sway
When the bridal gown came mama spit out the window
And a cop said, "The dog won't bite"
And the sad man saying, "They've forgotten when"
And the blood running black in the valley shadow
And the river running all the while

Yonder come a glad man singing a song
About a lover rolled over said, "You must be tired"
And the truth coming toward the light
About a sad man knocking on a chapel door
And a burned out boat called "tried by fire"
And the mouth of the river is wide

God Made the Automobile

God made the automobile
To pass all the pretty girls
That smoke by the side of the road
Their blues loving boys in tow
To drive until the end of the day
And bow to a borrowed flag
Beside all the brave and the blind
And men without men in mind

To pass all the things he made
But then never bothered to name
And no one will tell the truth
And no one will hide it from you
Like birds around the grave

God made the automobile
And I made a little boy
To pass all the blissfully young
The snake with a forked tongue
That preys on the wanting for time
And makes in the sleepless waves
The fear of the Black and the Jew
And blood for the camera crew

And passes the things he made
And then never bothers to name
And no one can tell the truth
And no one can hide it from you
Like birds around the grave

Godless Brother in Love

Godless brother in love
you might as well
Lay down that rose
and fold the flag
She hears money
and taps that broken freedom bell
See her big children
burning rags by the riverside
You can hear them
on the hilltop laughing
Cursing every bird in the air
Telling her what fun they're having
Driving eyes closed

Godless brother
as far as I can tell
The night won't compensate the blind
She looks lovely as lightning,
oh, but what the hell
Her big kids all run down the road
with no memories at all

And you can hear them
on the hilltop laughing
Cursing every bird in the air
Telling her what fun they're having
Driving eyes closed

Grace for Saints and Ramblers

There were banged up heads
stealing first base
Underneath the table
so we never said grace
Falling out of bed
for the workday week
There was kissing in the cracks
Of the flashflood street
There were budding blossoms
blaring Johnny Rotten
Chewed up and swallowed
By the prophet
they were trying to follow
Picked too green
and we paid no tax
On our quick romantic cul-de-sacs
But it all came down
to you and I

There were crashed out cars
in our bar code clothes
There was rubbing on each other
Rubbing ghost on ghost
There were junked up punks
and the Jesus freaks
Weaving in and out of trouble
Wrapping round and round a leash
There were sleepless dreamers,
doomsday preachers
The message and the messenger
The gun beneath the register
The sweet gum tree
by the tough drunk tank
We could never give enough
to the bad blood bank
There were hopeless sinners,
sweepstake winners
They danced with the farmer's daughter
Capered with the corporate lawyers
But it all came down to you and I

There was laughing in the light,
sugar in the shade
There were backstab handshakes
made on faith
We were never out of time
And we'd never entertain
Anybody say the habit of the wind
Was going to change
There were misled misfits,
teething biscuits
Fountains full of penny wishes
Potties full of pretty fishes
Side by side with the birds and bees
And they never said grace,
never ever took a knee
With the saints and ramblers,
movie star handlers
High above the aviary,
underneath the cemetery
And we never wondered why
Cause the sun was in our eyes
There was seed for the field
There was grease for the wheel
We were drinking with the luminaries
Eating with the missionaries
But it all came down to you and I

GRACE FOR SAINTS AND RAMBLERS

THERE WERE BANGED UP HEADS STEALING FIRST BASE
UNDERNEATH THE TABLE SO WE NEVER SAID GRACE
FALLING OUT OF BED FOR THE WORKDAY WEEK
THERE WAS KISSING IN THE CRACKS OF THE FLASHFLOOD STREET
THERE WERE BUDDING BLOSSOMS BLARING JOHNNY ROTTEN
CHEWED UP AND SWALLOWED BY THE PROPHET THEY WERE TRYING TO
FOLLOW
PICKED TOO GREEN AND WE PAID NO TAX ON OUR QUICK ROMANTIC
CUL DE SACS

BUT IT ALL CAME DOWN TO YOU AND I . . .
THERE WERE CRASHED OUT CARS IN OUR BARCODE CLOTHES
THERE WAS RUBBING ON EACH OTHER, RUBBING GHOST ON GHOST
THERE WERE JUNKED UP PUNKS AND THE JESUS FREAKS
WEAVING IN AND OUT OF TROUBLE, WRAPPING ROUND AND ROUND A
LEASH
THERE WERE SLEEPLESS DREAMERS, DOOMSDAY PREACHERS
THE MESSAGE AND THE MESSENGER, THE GUN BENEATH THE REGISTER
THE SWEET GUM TREE BY THE TOUGH DRUNK TANK
WE COULD NEVER GIVE ENOUGH TO THE BAD BLOOD BANK
THERE WERE HOPELESS SINNERS, SWEEPSTAKE WINNERS
THEY DANCED WITH THE FARMER'S DAUGHTER, CAPERED WITH THE
CORPORATE LAWYERS

BUT IT ALL CAME DOWN TO YOU AND I . . .
THERE WAS LAUGHING IN THE LIGHT, SUGAR IN THE SHADE
THERE WERE BACKSTAB HANDSHAKES MADE ON FAITH
WE WERE NEVER OUT OF TIME AND WE'D NEVER ENTERTAIN
ANYBODY SAY THE HABIT OF THE WIND WAS GONNA CHANGE
THERE WERE MISLEAD MISFITS, TEETHING BISCUITS
FOUNTAINS FULL OF PENNY WISHES, POTTIES FULL OF PRETTY FISHES
SIDE BY SIDE WITH THE BIRDS AND BEES
AND WE NEVER SAID GRACE, NEVER EVER TOOK A KNEE
WITH THE SAINTS AND RAMBLERS, MOVIE STAR HANDLERS
HIGH ABOVE THE AVIARY, UNDERNEATH THE CEMETARY
AND WE NEVER WONDERED WHY CAUSE THE SUN WAS IN OUR EYES
THERE WAS SEED FOR THE FIELD, THERE WAS GREASE FOR THE WHEEL
WE WERE DRINKING WITH LUMINARIES, EATEN WITH THE MISSIONARIES

BUT IT ALL CAME DOWN TO YOU AND I . . .

Grass Widows

We found each other blown between the trees
Waning moons wanting to be swallowed by the sea
Like we finally saw the colors of the world
We grew the garden snake within the weeds
Laid each other long across a flat backstreet
Like we finally saw the colors of the world

We felt the sun leave us for the west
Little lips always falling farther from the breast
Like we finally saw the colors of the world
We ran a white flag up the mast
Puckered up like a widow dreaming in the grass
Like we finally saw the colors of the world

Like we saw black
Like we saw black and blue
You pressed a pillow full of snow on my bruise
Like we saw black
Like we saw God green too
You saw it awful but it's over too soon

Like we saw black
Running around red ripe vines
I found you in the folds of lonely red night
Like we saw black
Lying in golden white light
Lonely so you tried to love me alright

We threw our money to the river stones
Led each other through the woods to wander back alone
Like we finally saw the colors of the world
We let the taste linger in the mouth
South Chicago never gave us more to sing about
Like we finally saw the colors of the world

Gray Stables

Brave lady, I could see you through the mosses
Laid, shameless in the sun
My lady with her porcelain and her weightless
Face, pleasing everyone

Gray stables and the horses of the righteous
Pray daily for the brave

Lady, you were gorgeous in your weakness
Wet flowers on the ground
My lady never told me of her sadness
Bones floating in the sound

Brave lady, could you see me in the darkness
Wait, nameless like a stone
My lady with her watches by the mattress
Bathes lately all alone

Gray stables and the horses of the righteous
Pray daily for the brave

Lady, would you love me if I left her
Laid breathless in the sun
My lady, like a teacup on the counter
Frail, pleasing everyone

IRON & WINE

Half Moon

Halfway home in the hilltop trees
And all our footprints in the snow
And the evening glow leaving

Low night noise in the wintertime
I wake beside you on the floor
Counting your breathing

I can't see nothing in this half moon
Lay me down if I should lose you

Halfway working on a worn out house
And all our friends the ragged crows
And aching bones whining

Where are we when the twilight comes
The darker valley and the breeze
And the frozen leaves chiming

Because I can't see nothing in this half moon
Lay me down if I should lose you

Halfway to Richmond

I'll make supper for myself
I'll watch the clock upon the shelf
I'll clean this broken house you denied
Is your time much better spent
by giving such a small percent
to every pleasantry that I've tried?

What's this ugly thing I see?
When was this cold and uncomely
Animosity begotten?
Fucking with the lights left on
'Til every ounce of strength was gone
Is this something you've forgotten?

When a new sun warms the bedroom wall
I'll be halfway to Richmond
I'm the fool just to care at all
You're the free vagabond

London Bridge is falling down
And Simon says to turn around
These games ain't too fun when you're grown
Where'd you go and why'd you leave?
I'll close my eyes and count to three
Then hurry up and wait by the phone

But when a new sun warms the bedroom wall
I'll be halfway to Richmond
I'm the fool just to care at all
You're the free vagabond

In the Reins (with Calexico)

Before I signed with Sub Pop, I was just getting to know Howard Greynolds, who became my manager. He suggested using Calexico as a backing band, my indie rock Sly & Robbie. I loved the idea, because I was a big fan. We didn't do it then, but it definitely stuck in my mind as a possibility.

Howard had a label called Overcoat Records, and a couple of years later he was doing a series of EPs where he paired artists together like Will Oldham and Tortoise. When he asked if Iron & Wine with Calexico could be part of that series, I was psyched. Even though I had been learning a lot about working in a studio, going to Tucson and playing with Joey Burns and John Convertino pushed me in directions that I would never have thought possible. Looking back, it had such an effect on me that it's hard to imagine what kind of music I would be making now if I hadn't experienced recording with them when I did.

Before then, I was just dabbling, experimenting. Music wasn't my thing—I'd gone to art school, not music school—and outside of a couple cowboy chords and an ear, I didn't have much to go on. All the musical experience Joey and John had—playing in Giant Sand, being on the road, playing and recording with so many different artists—there's stuff they taught me that I hadn't had access to before. All my recordings until then had been done a track at a time with overdubs, but when I got to Tucson, they were like, "All right, you're over there, I'm over here, John's over there, and we're gonna play the song now." As someone who liked to polish a thing until it shined before showing it to other people, it was horrifying to me, but they made it easy. No attitude, all encouragement. It was very free, and it all felt familiar really quickly. That was the first time I really understood the immediacy and magic of live takes, of being in the moment and trying to catch lightning in a bottle. It was empowering and inspiring. It set me on a different track.

The songs themselves were mostly written around the same time as the demos that became the first record. So in essence it was exactly what Howard and I had imagined a few years earlier, taking some of those demos and going into the studio with Joey and John. Choosing which ones to record in this context was a matter of picking through what I had and trying to find some kind of throughline. It seems silly, but I was thinking of Calexico as a Western band, so I picked "He Lays in the Reins" because it was a song with a horse in it! Anyway, it seemed like an easy place for us to come together, shake hands, and see where we went from there. All the others were added or discarded because of the way they related to that song. Mostly conventional, lovelorn Americana kind of songs.

I did the cover image on the kitchen table in Miami. It's mixed media, a painting on top of a photograph that I'd taken at this ranch near Santa Fe where we had some friends. Since "He Lays in the Reins" was always the centerpiece in my mind, I felt like the image should reflect that. There was a lot of watercolor involved, but I tend to use whatever's around. With the kids being little then, a lot of crayons. Probably some applesauce in there somewhere.

He Lays in the Reins

One more drink tonight,
let your gray stallion rest
Where he lays in the reins
For all of the speed and the strength he gave

One more kiss tonight,
from some tall stable girl
She's like grace from the earth
when you're all tuckered out and tame

Nunca pense que jamas
Tener la oportunindad de reencontrar
el camino de Nuevo
Para formar un mundo mejor

One more tired thing,
a gray moon on the rise
When your want from the day
Makes you to curse
in your sleep at night

With one more gift to bring,
we may well find you
Laid like your steed in his reins
Tangled too tight
and too long to fight

Hearts Walk Anywhere

A lover taught me this song
Hearts walk anywhere
The autumn leaves
The aster blooms
Years are never enough

Light is what to believe
Rain runs in your hand
A house falls down
Birds come back
A lover taught me this song

The wind is given to tears
Laugh your lover awake
Waning moons
Teach the weeds
Years are never enough

Hickory

He kissed her once
as she leaned on the windowsill
She'll never love him
but knows that her father will
Her fallen fruit
is all rotten in the middle
But her breast never dries when he's hungry

The money came
and she died in her rocking chair
The window wide
and the rain in her braided hair
A letter locked in
the pattern of her knuckle
Like a hymn to the house she was making

We're blind and whistling,
just around the corner
And there's a wind that is
whispering something
We're strong as hell but not hickory rooted

She kissed him once
'cause he gave her a cigarette
Then turned around but he waits
like a turned down bed
And summer left like her
walking with another
And the sound of the church bell ringing

The money came
and he died like a butterfly
A buried star in the haze
of the city lights
A gun went off
and a mother dropped her baby
On a blue feathered wing, we were lucky

We're blind and whistling,
just around the corner
And there's a wind
that is whispering something
We're strong as hell but not hickory rooted

A History of Lovers

Louise only got from me innocent poetry
Although she played to not listen
But still I can hear myself speak as if no one else
Ever could offer the same

Some say she knowingly tastes like a recipe
All those so foolish and willing
I said, "Babe, I can picture you bend as if wanting to
Bow as the curtain goes down"

Cuddle some men, they'll remember you bitterly
Fuck 'em, they'll come back for more
I asked my Louise, would she leave and so, cripple me
Then came a knock at the door

I came for my woman, he came with a razor blade
Bound like us all for the ocean
I hope that she's happy, I'm blamed for the death
Of a man who would take her from me

Some say they saw in me innocent poetry
Some say they'll never be certain
But still it's been written, a history of lovers
In giving and taking, and ink

Cuddle some men, they'll remember you fittingly
Cut 'em, they'll come back for more
I asked my Louise, would she leave and so, cripple me
Then came the knock at the door

Louise came to rescue me, missing the irony
Blood made her heart change its beating
I hope that she's happy I'm blamed for the death
Of a man she found better than me

Homeward, These Shoes

Homeward, the new road meanders
Washed out, the old road asks, "What did I bring?"
Flowers, a verse about springtime
Perchance, in the tree line, she's awaiting for me
Homeward, these shoes worn to paper
Thin as the reason I left here so young
Homeward, and what if I see her
There in the doorway I walked away from?
White house asleep on the hillside
Firm as a habit I struggle to shed
Homeward with heaven above me
Old road behind me, a door up ahead

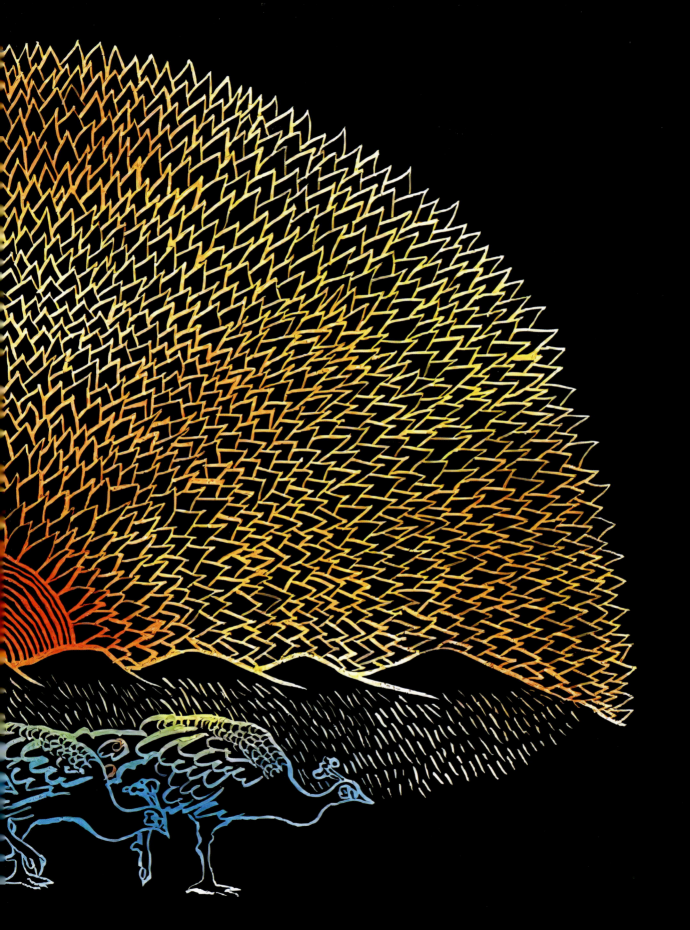

House by the Sea

There is a house by the sea
Two jealous sisters,
there waiting for me
And one is laid on the floor
One is changing
the locks on her doors
But I've been buying
their time on my knees
And I've been selling them
blankets to bleed on

Around the house by the sea
The scent of roses
and raspberry leaves
And there is smoke
in my clothes
Too much time with just
smoke in my nose
But I've been making
the meaning they lack
And I've been burning
that book they come back to

There is a house by the sea
And an ocean
between it and me
And like the shape of a wave
The jealous sisters
will sing on my grave
I've been living
to run where they've led
And I've been dying
to rise from their bed
But I've been sparing
my neck from their chain
And they've been changing
the sound of my name
And I've been swimming
to them in my sleep
But I've been dreaming
our love and our freedom

In Your Own Time

In your own time
you'll drink something evil
Sing like an old crow
and worship the land
Don't be scared
if I walk with the devil
Run down the mountain
and ask for your hand

'Cause we only want a life
that's well worth living
Sleeping's no kind of life at all

Come meet the family
and sit by the fire
Someone will catch you,
if you want to fall

In your own time
you'll dance in the moonlight
Smoke like a freight train
and fuck like a dog
Don't be scared
if I tell you I love you
I'll be good to you
and then I'll be gone

Cause we only want a life
that's well worth living
And sleeping ain't no kind
of life at all

Come meet the family
and get warm by the fire
Someone will catch you
if you want to fall

Innocent Bones

Cain got a milk-eyed mule from the auction
Abel got a telephone
And even the last of their blue eyed babies know

That the burning man is the color of the end of day
And how every tongue that gets bit
Always has another word to say

Cain bought a blade from some witch at the window
Abel bought a bag of weed
And even the last of their brown eyed babies see

That the cartoon king has a tattoo of a bleeding heart
There ain't a penthouse Christian wants the pain of the scab
But they all want the scar
How every mouth sings of what it's without
So we all sing of love
And how it ain't one dog who's good at fucking
And denying who he's thinking of

Cain heard a cat tumble limp off the rooftop
Abel heard his papa pray
That even their last of their black-eyed babies say

That every saint has a chair you can borrow
And a church to sell
And that the wind blows cold across the back
Of the master and the kitchen help
There's a big pile of innocent bones
Still holding up the garden wall
And it was always the broken hand
We learned to lean on after all
How God knows if Christ came back
He would find us in a poker game
After finding out the drinks were all free
But they won't let you out the door again

Jesus the Mexican Boy

Jesus the Mexican boy
born in a truck on the fourth of July
gave me a card with a lady naked on the back
Barefoot at night on the road
Fireworks blooming above in the sky
I never knew I was given the best one from the deck

He never wanted nothing I remember
Maybe a broken bottle if I had two
Hanging behind his holy even temper
Hiding the more unholy things I'd do

Jesus the Mexican boy
Gave me a ride on the back of his bike
Out to the fair though I welched on a five dollar bet
Drunk on calliope songs
We met a home-wrecking carnival girl
He's never asked for a favor or the money yet

Jesus the Mexican boy
Born in a truck on the fourth of July
I fell in love with his sister unrepentantly
Fearing he wouldn't approve
We made a lie that was feeble at best
Boarded a train bound for Vegas and married secretly

I never gave him nothing, I remember
Maybe gave a broken bottle, if I had two
Hanging behind his holy even temper
Hiding the more unholy things I do

Jesus the Mexican boy
Wearing a long desert trip on his tie
Low and behold he was standing under the welcome sign
Naked the Judas in me
Fell by the tracks but he lifted me high
Kissing my head like a brother and never asking why

Jezebel

Who's seen Jezebel?
She was born to be the woman I would know
And hold like the breeze
Half as tight as both eyes closed

Who's seen Jezebel?
She went walking where the cedars line the road
Her blouse on the ground
Where the dogs were hungry, roaming

Saying, "Wait, we swear
We'll love you more and wholly
Jezebel, it's we that you are for only"

Who's seen Jezebel?
She was born to be the woman we could blame
Make me a beast half as brave
I'd be the same

And who's seen Jezebel?
She was gone before I ever got to say
"Lay here my love
You're the only shape I'll pray to, Jezebel"

Who's seen Jezebel?
Will the mountain last as long as I can wait
Wait for the dawn
How it aches to meet the day

Who's seen Jezebel?
She was certainly the spark for all I've done
The window was wide
She could see the dogs come running

Saying, "Wait, we swear
We'll love you more and wholly
Jezebel, it's we that you are for only"

WHO'S SEEN JEZABEL?

WAIT WE SWEAR TO LOVE YOU

AND ~~WHOLLY~~ WHOLLY MORE JEZEBEL

ITS WE THAT YOU ARE fo~~r~~

MIDNIGHT

~~REALLY~~ ONLY

THERES A SNAKE ACROSS THE TRAILER HITCH

WHO'S SEEN JEZEBELLE?
I WENT CALLING BY THE CEDARS (BY THE RO
CALLING AND CRYING MY JEZEBELLE, DON'T GO

WHO'S SEEN JEZEBELLE

SHE WAS BORN TO BE THE WOMAN I WOULD KNOW
AND ~~HOLD~~ HOLD LIKE THE BREEZE ~~ONLY~~ HALF AS TIGHT
~~AS~~ AS BOTH EYES CLOSED

AND WHO'S SEEN JEZEBELLE?

SHE WENT WALKING WHERE THE CEDARS LINE THE ROA

WHERE
HER BLOUSE ON THE GROUND ~~AND~~ THE DOGS

WERE
~~ALL~~ HUNGRY, ROAMING

SLEEP WELL, JEZABEL

WILL ~~IT~~ THE MOUNTAIN LAST~~S~~ AS LONG AS I CAN WAIT

~~WAIT~~ LIKE A SOLDIER, THE ~~DRUMS~~

~~SO NEAR AND RUMBLING~~
WAIT LIKE THE DAWN HOW IT ACHES TO ~~MAKE~~ MEET
THE DAY

~~AND WE'LL WAIT UNTIL SUMMER COMES~~

~~SHE WAS~~ ~~GONE BEFORE~~ THE GARDEN WALL ~~WAS~~ DONE
~~BORN~~
SHE WAS ~~BORN TO~~ BE THE ~~FOOL~~ for ALL I'VE
CERTAINLY   SPARK
THE WINDOW WAS ~~WIDE~~ SHE COULD SEE THE DOGS
~~WHO WILL~~   COME RUNNING
SINGING...

~~WHO'S SEEN JEZEBELLE~~

WHO'S SEEN JEZEBELLE?
~~THERE'S A DIRT TRACK~~
THERE'S A DIRT TRACK ~~IN~~ THROUGH THE CHAIN LINK
BY THE ROAD
A BLOUSE ON THE GROUND AND TWO DOGS
THAT I DON'T KNOW

WHO'S SEEN JEZEBELLE
SHE WAS BORN TO BE THE WOMAN WE COULD BLAME
MAKE ME A BEAST HALF AS BRAVE

I'D BE THE SAME

AND WHO'S SEEN JEZEBELLE?

SHE WAS GONE BEFORE I EVER GOT TO SAY

AY HERE MY LOVE, YOU'RE THE ONLY SHAPE

I'LL PRAY TO

John's Glass Eye

John don't see well in the evenings
Because of his one glass eye
That he got just as Martha was leaving
Shot him instead of saying goodbye

Though the door took the brunt of the buckshot
Scattered on the right of his face
He was blind to the traveling clothes she'd bought
When she caught him down at Lucy's place

Joy

Deep inside the heart
of this troubled man
There's an itty bitty boy
tugging hard at your hand
Born bitter as a lemon
but you must understand
That you've been bringing me joy

And I'll only lie when you
don't want the truth
I'm only frightened 'cause you
finally gave me something to lose
And it's as loud as a thunderclap
and you hear it too
But you've been bringing me joy

Deep inside the heart
of this crazy mess
I'm only calm when I get lost
within your wilderness
Born crooked as a creek bed
and come to confess
That you've been bringing me joy

And when I'm alive,
I'm living for you
Another bluebird dying
but for singing the blues
And it's a heartfelt silly sort of bumbling tune
About how you're bringing me joy

Judgement

Day walks out and there's no sound
There's a candle burning by me now
Light enough for to see the things beyond me
The door is wide as her eyes on me
So the night comes in and starts to breathe
The only name that I really know

Tell me, dear, do you think of me
At a drop of rain or when you see
Wind that rakes as it moves across the water?
Judgement comes when I'm all alone
Like a spyglass on the furthest coast
Favored now that it's left behind

When you talk to me
You could swallow me

Nighttime brings me a place I fear
Where I hear your words and feel you near
Fingers only to find a frozen memory
Sometimes clothes chosen long ago
Or directions down a gravel road
Make you wish you could take them back

Days walk on and when there's no sound
I go straight to you and find you down
Kneeling next to the water where I left you
Knee deep now in the creek I made
From a landscape lost, but want to save
Save it now or be punished more

When you talk to me
You could swallow me

Nighttime brings a place I fear
Where I hear your words and feel you near
Fingers never to find a warmer memory
Sometimes friends we knew long ago
Or affections we set free to go
Find you right where you ran to hide

The Shepherd's Dog

When the album came out, I said it was like my version of Tom Waits's *Swordfishtrombones*. To my mind, that meant the moment he took a bit of a left turn after making several clever beatnik piano jazz records in the seventies. I felt like this was my moment to take that kind of a chance—and if I didn't take it, I was going to regret it.

I had set up a studio at the house near Austin. The idea was to have a place where I could dabble: record things, then go back and change them. Just like writing a song, where you write things down, then go back and scratch them out. When you're in the studio, time is always the biggest thing you're worried about. Since I could record at my house, I wasn't on the clock anymore. It comes with the curse that you feel like you're never finished, but it was great for me at the time.

I had enjoyed the space, the sparseness of the early records. I felt like what the songs were talking about and my minimalistic approach shook hands really easily—the aesthetics complemented each other. But they also had that space in part because I didn't understand how to do much else. The experience of playing with Calexico—both in the studio and on the road—had empowered me, allowed me to hear my voice in other sonic atmospheres. Now I felt like there were other things I wanted to say, other sounds I wanted to try, and so we just kind of let loose and did a lot of experimenting.

Most of it was done at the house. Joey Burns came out. Paul Niehaus brought his pedal steel. We'd met Rob Burger at a Neil Young tribute concert in New York where he was part of the band. We hit it off, so I asked him to come out.

We ended up doing sort of a hybrid thing where I would record the basic tracks at home—guitar, singing, maybe some drum stuff—and then when we needed some special sauce, we'd go back to Chicago and have people like Matt Lux and Jim Becker come in.

This record was the first one where I felt like I was wearing all my influences on my sleeve at the same time, and it made a cacophonous mess. Folk and dub, West African and Brazilian music, even boogie-woogie! All of it. Another part of it was that I was discovering what went into making my favorite records. You know, it's one thing to love the Beatles, which I always did, but now when I listened to the Beatles, there was a new curiosity about how they were doing what they were doing. So that was on my mind. And of course, at that time, Radiohead was on everyone's mind.

I was also reading Allen Ginsberg. I'm usually reading a lot of different poets, but this was the first time I'd really embraced and related to the Beat poet thing. The anger, the joy, and the confusion. His way of listing subjects and observations is relentless and chaotic and beautiful, like Whitman. And the effect of him repeating these religious-like mantras is disorienting and ecstatic and strange.

    The earlier songs were simpler, more clearly story songs, with an obvious beginning and end. These ones got darker, brooding, and psychedelic. Whenever there's a comforting image, there's usually some menace close behind. Also, where the other records articulated a search for wisdom, for solace, this one didn't seem worried about comforting anybody. I found it's much more fun to write for the bad guy than the good guy.

    It also had to do with me. I'm not a terribly active person politically, but before this I'd been actively inactive. *Who cares?* I thought. *We don't have any control over what happens.* I was complacent. During the first Bush administration, all my friends were lefties, so I thought everyone was like me, unhappy with what was going on. In my entire social circle, the discontentment was so consistent that I naively figured he would lose the next election. So when he won the second term, this new creeping sense of unease set in. I woke up and found that everything wasn't the way I thought it was. That shook me up. I felt like I'd left a cocoon and my senses were awake and engaged. It was an interesting place to land. I was an artist whose creative expression was usually about finding and creating comfort, and I was discovering that sometimes the most honest statement you can make is about how uncomforted you feel.

    It's there in "Boy with a Coin." I had this image of God leaving the Earth and talking to us from afar. He's not here. He's circling around out there somewhere. Did we do something wrong? Was He never really here to begin with? Regardless, it's an unsettled feeling. "Flightless Bird" is similar. It's a rite of passage song. That was me, waking up a man-boy in America with all it offers, good and bad. I remember working on it in the backyard in Miami and seeing a rat on the power lines. That made its way into the song: "watching the warm poison rats curl through the wide fence cracks." You know they're going to get in. You can't stop them. They're coming.

Kicking the Old Rain

Before you walk too far
Watching the sunlight leave
Kicking the old rain down the road
Teasing the rooftop birds
Laying some love by mine
Tired from laughing and trading tears

Know that our world is always on fire
Always a quiet pile of stones
We all float away with birthday balloons
Sing with your teeth and cross your heart

If you've been emptied out
Blowing the flowers around
Here comes another thunderhead
Its wind is a welcome green
Ask if it brought a song
You got a good one from the moon

Kingdom of the Animals

Jenny was gone and the moon blooms all shining
As we dragged our panic up and down the riverbed
Sweating wild and weird in our Sunday clothes

Jenny was gone though I thought that I knew her
And the rain came howling out of Virginia
Bluetick blowing the water out her nose

Jenny and me in the front row and singing
About how heaven calls the kingdom of the animals
All and all revealed to us one day

Jenny and me on the hilltop and peeking
At all their upturned bottles, jumping like leopards
Jaw harp teasing the brushfire in its rage

Jenny came back and the wet road still shining
In our eyes, an angel clear and coronal
Clothed in all that's prodigal and strange

Jenny came back and I thought that I heard her
Murmur something about "no men in Virginia"
Spat on the ground like a letter tossed away

Jenny and me in my dead truck and turning
Over just where heaven calls the kingdom of the animals
Scratching our heads where the wolf would go to lay

Jenny and me as the moon blooms were closing
And both her wide-eyed brothers running like shepherds
Dreaming the heat of the fields all in flames

Last Night

It's all that we do
It's all we don't
Reach deep in
each other's tears
Let them rumble and come
When they come in
their long waves
It's our last night
to lie in these arms

It's the giving the wind
all it wants
The turn after turn
until we're lost
And it's what we believe
in the limbs of hometown trees

When we let go
We'll disappear
It's our last night
to lie in these arms

It's the finding our clothes
behind the door
Dreaming a light
in our dark house
The sound of our hearts
Cars passing by
It's our last night
to lie in the arms

REINS   TRAPEZE 4
SODOM   WOMAN 4
FEVER   NAKED 4
WOMAN   PAGAN 6
LION   UPWARD 5
UPWARD   HISTORY 2
MARY ANNE   FEVER 2
NAKED   LION 6
TRAPEZE   REINS 4
BIRD   GLAD 1
JEZEBEL   JEZEBEL 5
HISTORY   SODOM 2
FLIGHTLESS   FLIGHTLESS 5
PAGAN   SODOM
    FLIGHTLESS

7/9/09. OTTAWA BLUES FEST

---

sheraton.com   1 800 325 3535

SUCH
WOMAN
REINS
SODOM
JEZEBEL
DIE
FLIGHTLESS
UPWARD
BOY
FERN
NAKED
TRAPEZE

EACH COMING NIGHT
RESURRECTION FERN
PEACE BENEATH THE
     CITY
SODOM SOUTH GEORGIA
WOMAN KING
— WOLVES
CAROUSEL
HOUSE BY THE SEA
DEVIL NEVER SLEEPS
— PAGAN ANGEL
UPWARD OVER THE
     MOUNTAIN.
— TRAPEZE SWINGER

SODOM
WOMAN
UPWARD
REINS
NAKED
PEACE
MARY ANNE
TRAPEZE
VIGILANTES
FLIGHTLESS

Last of Your Rock 'n' Roll Heroes

Someday you're doing your thing
Someday you blame it on the company
And a couple of drinks
Like the last of your
rock 'n' roll heroes are gone

Someday you say what you feel
Someday you say it just to feel
Another hand on the wheel
Like the last of your
rock 'n' roll heroes are gone

Someday you walk in your shoes
Someday you're tired of the kind of nothing
You've got to lose
Like the last of your
rock 'n' roll heroes are gone

Someday you're making a fist
Someday you give away everything
Until you know what to miss
Like the last of your
rock 'n' roll heroes are gone

Someday you're headed back home
Someday you wade into that water
Because you're sinking for stone
Like the last of your
rock 'n' roll heroes are gone

Someday you turn to your friends
Someday they know why you stood up
And turned into the wind
Like the last of your
rock 'n' roll heroes are gone

Lean into the Light

We're not happy
most of the time
But we're not
sad too often
We'll keep walking
blind in the sun
While the rain is falling

But we'll laugh
by the raging riverside
Laugh just as long as
we're side by side
Laugh as we lean
into the light

We're no better off
than we were
But we're no worse
for trying
We'll keep walking
blind by the graves
And all the church bells chiming

And we'll laugh as the tears
roll from our eyes
Laugh holding hands
and our knuckles white
Laugh as we lean into the light

Every morning,
every goodnight
For every wrong word
our mouths can make
We say a couple right
Every welcome,
every goodbye
For every dark move
our bodies make
We're leaning towards the light

Lion's Mane

Run like a race for family
When you hear like you're alone
The rusty gears of morning
And faceless, busy phones
We gladly run in circles
But the shape we meant to make is gone

And love is a tired symphony
You hum when you're awake
And love is a crying baby
Mama warned you not to shake
And love's the best sensation
Hiding in the lion's mane

So I'll clear the road, the gravel
And the thorn bush in your path
It burns a scented oil
That I'll drip into your bath
The water's there to warm you
And the earth is warmer when you laugh

And love is the scene I render
When you catch me wide awake
And love is the dream you enter
Though I shake and shake and shake you
And love's the best endeavor
Waiting in the lion's mane

Loaning Me Secrets

One drop of poison spilled on your gown
One drop of danger set your legs running

Don't kiss a leper by closing one eye
Don't give a hand to one you can't follow

But you know I saved everything you gave to me
When we shared a bed and you were loaning me secrets

Don't break a bottle stumbling around
Don't cut yourself and bleed on a stranger

Keep looking forward, chin in the air
I'll watch your back from the far horizon

But just know I'll save everything you gave to me
When we shared a bed and you were loaning me secrets

Loretta

Look at the shadow on our tree
Seems a mean early dusk
Loretta looked up, the gray sky low
Two by two on the bus

Water and anger in our house
Though she spoke of rainbows
Reaching the roof with soaking shoes
Rivers up, where'd she go?

You're wiser, Loretta
You're wiser and only twenty-five

Chair and the TV floating by
Through our room and out the door
Loretta she prayed for what to do
If it rained anymore

She was a washcloth wet with love
I was not, she was mine
I'm in the olive tree next door
Rivers up to my eyes

You're wiser, Loretta
Much wiser and only just in time

Loud as Hope

Darling, behave
though your boy is gone
Or so we've heard
Ophelia would rise
if it was her song
And say these words
"Summer comes
with its color on
To take your breath away
Winter turns all the summer's
love to gray"

Darling, behave
though the barnyard
Won't say where he's gone
Ophelia would sing
if the orchard let her
What went wrong
"Summer comes yelling
loud as hope
And takes your breath away
Winter takes what the summer
had to say"

Love and Some Verses

Love is a dress that you made
Long to hide your knees
Love to say this to your face
"I'll love you only"
For your days and excitement
What will you keep for to wear?
Someday drawing you different
May I be weaved in your hair?

Love and some verses you hear
Say what you can't say
Love to say this in your ear
"I'll love you that way"
From your changing contentments
What will you choose for to share?
Someday drawing you different
May I be weaved in your hair?

LOVE AND A DRESS
THAT YOU MADE ~~HEMMED ABOUT YOUR~~ *TO SHOW YOUR*
~~SHARP ~~THIS~~ OF THE WARM SEA~~
LONG TO HIDE YOUR KNEES
LOVE TO SAY THIS
TO YOUR FACE
"I'll LOVE YOU ONLY"
FOR YOUR DAYS AND EXCITEMENT
WHAT WILL YOU KEEP FOR TO WEAR
SOMEDAY, DRAWING *YOU* ~~US~~ DIFFERENT
~~BE STILL~~ BE WEAVED IN YOUR HAIR
MAY I

~~LOVE AND THE CONCH AND~~
~~WAS BLACK~~
~~MOON LIKE A CHALK LINE~~

~~LOVE AND THE DRESS~~
~~THAT YOU SAVED~~
~~DAD AND THE CHEAP RING~~

LOVE AND SOME VERSES
YOU HEAR
SAY WHAT YOU CAN'T SAY
LOVE TO SAY THIS
IN YOUR EAR
"I'll LOVE YOU THAT WAY"
FROM YOUR CHANGING CONTENTMENTS
WHAT WILL YOU CHOOSE FOR TO SHARE
SOMEDAY, DRAWING YOU DIFFERENT
MAY I BE WEAVED IN YOUR HAIR

Lovesong of the Buzzard

In the failing light
of the afternoon
Lucy in the shade
of the dogwood blooms
Yesterday, the solace
of a poison fish
Tomorrow I'll be kissing
on her blood red lips

And no one is the savior
they would like to be
The love song of the buzzard
in the dogwood tree
With a train of horses laughing
through the traffic light
And the cradle's unimaginative
sense of time

Springtime and the promise
of an open fist
A tattoo of a flower
on a broken wrist
Lucy tells me jokingly
to "wipe her brow
with a pocket map to heaven"
and the sun goes down

Lovers' Revolution

I came to you and you to me
And we were tapping on the window at the children
when the piggy bank broke
And pitching quite a fit
About how the makers of the medicine
will always say you're looking sick

I came to you and you to me
And we would whimper to the women
washing milk off of their formal white clothes
But the funny thing
Was how when god was in his people,
we were dreaming about who else to be
And all the fingers that we damaged
when all we wanted was the diamond ring

I came to you and you to me
And we were barking at the drug dogs,
blood dried black on their hands
And never realized
You never tussle with a giant
'til you can hit him right between the eyes
And that no matter how we chewed it,
we'd be choking on a comprise
'Cause all the jaws,
all the claws lay restless by the riverside
And it wasn't muscle in the shadow
that was shoving us into the light

I came to you and you to me
And we were snatching at a war baby's bottle
just to trade it for change
But now it's come to pass

That every eye beneath the mountain
saw the smoke but no one heard the blast
That no one knew the arm was broken
although everybody signed the cast
And until the government was good,
she said, "Man, I thought you'd never ask"
That when love wore out her welcome
they just booked her for a bag of grass
That while she cried on the cross,
we were sucking on the laughing gas
And when the head had left the body,
not a flag was hanging half-mast

I came to you and you to me
And then we lost our own lovers' revolution
but it started again
And now we're one

One of the parade wake widows
walking home into the setting sun
One of the soldiers lost in the dreams
that never lose the gun
One of the wise men wandering
the podium without a tongue
One of the trophies tarnished by the mess
we made of being young
One of the prayers, one of the promises
swallowed with our chewing gum
One of the deaf ears, dumber all the time
for all the years of drums
One of the wide-eyed soap boxes
buried under Washington
One of the beat cops combing
every sidewalk crack for love
One of the crowded stars uncounted
when the map was done
One of the withered in the garden
left to wonder when the rain will come

Low Light
Buddy of Mine

He's in a white car waiting for the light to change
He's a buddy of mine but I can't complain
He can make a lot of money, he can touch his toes
He knows you never look until the lights are low
But I love you and you love me
So we never demand and we never agree
I love you and you love me
And there's new fruit humming in the old fruit trees

He's in a white car waiting in a parking lot
And he's jealous of me and what we've got
He can buckle his belt, he can shine his shoe
But he could never end up where I found you
And I love you and you love me
So we don't talk back and we don't say please
I love you and you love me
And there's new fruit humming in the old fruit trees

He's in a white car waiting for the rain to pass
He's a buddy of mine but that won't last
Because he ain't the dumb grin on an empty cup
We both took him for when he showed up
Because I love you and you love me
So we both get stuck and we both get free
I love you and you love me
And there's new fruit humming in the old fruit trees

Me and Lazarus

Me and Lazarus
We shoveled all the ashes out
Black bed linens blowing around
Back and forth and up and down
Guess I had nowhere else to go

Me and Lazarus
Kept bailing out that riverboat
Floating by the choir robes
Bobbing in the ebb and flow
Guess I had nowhere else to go

He's an emancipated punk
and he can dance
But he's got a hole in the pocket
of his pants
Must be a symptom of
outstanding circumstances

Me and Lazarus
Fed her with a baby spoon
Fever flowing through the room
Far too long and way to soon
Guess I had nowhere else to go

Me and Lazarus
We picked up papa's white boy blues
Hand-me-downs and Sunday shoes
But never made the local news
Guess I had nowhere else to go

And I'm a liberated loser
that can roll
But where my pocket was
I'm peeking through a hole
A couple second chances
surely would console me

Milkweed

Always coming back
Coming back for something
Back for something
Always coming back
Coming back for something
Back for something

Always coming back with the butterflies
Breakfast on the table
Backseat full of baby shoes
A pile of jumper cables

Always coming back
Coming back for something
Back for something
Rain falls all around the world
Summer leaves afraid of changing
Coming back for something
Back for something
There's something carved in our hearts for good
Something always fading

God of the dollar's a god of fear
The guns on the TV really get you
Kiss me again in a street light
Coming on

The el train rattles back and forth
A body takes a beating
Milkweed is for the butterflies
Promises are for keeping

Always coming back
Coming back for something
Back for something
Always coming back
Coming back for something
Back for something

Minor Piano Keys

Say, say something nice to her
Fragrant and sturdier
Delicate hands for shoulders sliding down
Days, days like a summer rain
Blink and they're gone again
Soaking, she sits alone outside and now

Prays, prays for her solider boy
In fire and angry noise
Under the thumb of the Lord
And waits, quilting and quietly
The minor piano keys
Slip the screen on the door

Say, say what you mean to her
Washing her colander
Eyes on the stranger cresting around the bend
Days, days like the winter snow
Linger 'til heaven knows
Naked, she sings the table grace and then

Prays, prays for her solider boy
In fire and angry noise
Under the thumb of the Lord
And waits, quilting and quietly
The minor piano keys
Slip the screen on the door

Miss Bottom of the Hill

So miss bottom of the hill what do you want?
The sun is shining and your lovers
Always lose you in the dark
And they've all chosen to remember
How the sparrows hit the window
That you close to keep the cat out in the yard

And like your body being dragged behind the moon
You bring a memory of your mother
Like the money in your shoe
And how her penetrating wisdom
Her bulletproof religion
Always rip you like good wool off of the loom

You've floated farther than you ever meant to go
And only now see you were naked
When the wind began to blow
There's no advice that you've been missing
No trespass unforgiven
Just a river with no pity for your boat

I've come to know that I was stealing
All your kisses on the evening
The dogs were loose and lying in the street
You've learned to blend into the choir
How to hold your hand in fire
And what to say instead of what you mean
With the trouble it saves for just how hard it can be

You've met the women gluing jewels onto a crown
You know men hiding in the city
And their way of being found
And you've got nothing on your shoulders
Still there's nothing too much colder
Than the rubble of a house that's fallen down

And like a baby crying until it falls asleep
The autumn's over by the time
You count the color of the leaves
You're painting buzzards on the ceiling
Falling faithless at the healing
With your friends around you wailing on their knees

And I've come to know that I was stealing
All your kisses on the evening
The fog had swallowed everything but us
You've learned to balance on the cable
Drink us all under the table
And who to try instead of who you trust
With the hand on your heart that threw you under the bus

So miss bottom of the hill what do you want?
The sun is shining and you've cleaned
Your pretty pistol of a heart
But when you talk about tomorrow
When to beg and when to borrow
It's how to hit the ground before you hear the shot

And like a fish too deep and drifting in the sea
You've grown accustomed to the blindness
Looking up and anxiously
But there's a stone inside your pocket
While you're plowing through the market
Though you know even the time it takes ain't free

And I've come to know that I was stealing
All your kisses on the evening
The stars were barely hanging in the sky
You've learned to eat when you're not hungry
How to laugh when nothing's funny
And what to get instead of getting by
But oh how it changes with the passing of time

You've heard so many voices hidden in the wind
See all the children of the world
And how its fingers reach for them
Two branches tired of their bending
I don't see our story ending
Quite as clean as it was easy to begin

And like a hole that let the fox under the fence
You've got no solace and no sanctuary
You can recommend
Begging for mercy at the bedside
We got frozen in the headlights
But our kind of mercy never made much sense

Continued on page 158

And I've come to know that I was stealing
All your kisses on the evening
We both were disappearing in the waves
You've learned to lead the one you follow
How to spit out what you swallow
And when to hint instead of give away
That secret of ours is one I'll take to the grave

And so miss bottom of the hill what do you want?
The sun is shining and I think
You want me more often than not
But like your father in the garden
I won't finish what I started
Until you bill me for the flowers I forgot

And like a curse too old for anyone to care
You said to meet you on the mountain
'Cause you'd never make it there
And sucked your thumb along the highway
Proudly promising that one day
I'd miss the way we tumbled down the stairs

And I've come to know that I was stealing
All your kisses on the evening
The car was gently gliding off the road
You've learned to rise above your body
How to never say you're sorry
And where to go instead of going home
With the light by the bed
and all the clothes you've outgrown

Kiss Each Other Clean

I remember feeling conscious of trying new things. I was very aware of the possibility of getting stuck in a certain sound that people expected of me, and deathly afraid to be pigeonholed, so I was doing my best to keep pushing forward and wrestle my way out of that. The history of most bands is that they last maybe two or three years, then they're gone. I'd fallen into music so serendipitously that I was convinced the whole experiment was going to disappear. So before it did, I wanted to show everybody all my cards, let my creative flag fly.

I just wanted to mess with people's expectations, I think—for better or for worse—including my own expectations maybe most of all. Plus, I was playing with people who could play all kinds of music that I never could, which allowed me to follow the muse wherever it led. I was trying everything that I've ever been interested in, musically, all at the same time.

I was in constant working mode then, because I had the means—the studio at the house—and I had the motivation. There were so many songs that we even toyed with the idea of putting out a double album. This was around the time that streaming came about, so I had access to all the music that I remembered from growing up. I was listening to a lot of seventies AM radio pop. It was a nostalgic trip for me to absorb that music again—everything from Carly Simon to the Cornelius Brothers and Sister Rose, wonderful one-hit wonder kind of things that you'd see on an infomercial for the Super Hits of the seventies on cassette.

I think that contributed to the singability of this record. Where *Shepherd's Dog* was experimental but rooted in folk and blues, this one was taking that sonic palette and just doing pop songs. "Tree by the River" has that pop element. I'd had that melody banging around for years and I always liked it, but it seemed saccharine. There wasn't enough contradiction or complexity. It was in the bunch of songs that are on the *Archive Series Vol. 5: Tallahassee Recordings*, but it took me a long time to finish it. I had to infuse a little cruelty into it, like the line at the end: "I was coy in the half moon / happy just to be with you / and you were happy for me." It's like a Venus flytrap. The song draws you in with its sweetness, and then it's got you.

With a song like "Monkeys Uptown," I was definitely trying to do my version of Eddy Grant's "Electric Avenue." "Your Fake Name Is Good Enough for Me" started as a mashup of blues and African music—but with a Frank Zappa horn section—and wound up sounding like a weird show tune with an outro that channels Neil Young and Crazy Horse!

 The sound is more polished, but the lyrics mine similar territory to what was started with *Shepherd's Dog*, story songs in varying shades of light and dark that dream of being poems. I can be very impatient. I remember early on when I'd sit down with the guitar, I'd think, *I'm going to get another song today*. With that way of thinking, you end up doing something quickly that works. It's fine, but it's not really about enjoying *songwriting*, it's enjoying *having a song*. Later, I started to understand the importance of digging in, of sitting and humming a thing forever until a word pops out, then you start building. That kind of patience is contrary to how I've approached most of my life, but after doing it long enough I realized the rewards.

 Often I would find a refrain and then just expand on it. "Walking Far from Home" is one. Once I found that refrain, I could say anything. "I was walking far from home, I saw . . ." and just start listing. That's the model for lots of folk music, really. And if you're a daydreamer like me, you can sit forever and keep coming up with images or scenarios that expand on the phrase. It can be really freeing and fun. The difficult part is just keeping the inner critic at bay. Then, once you have that big bolt of cloth, you tailor it down into the little suit jacket of the song. Most good writing is rewriting, after all. And that's just how my brain works. My first ideas are not the most interesting, but they'll get me on a path to somewhere else. I think most people are like that.

 The idea behind the drawing that became the album cover was that sort of project we all did in elementary school, where you color a page with crayon, then cover it with black paint, and finally scratch out an image to reveal the color again. The peacocks and flowers create this exotic atmosphere, there's a burning barn in the background, and I'm wading in the river for redemption. That was the feeling of the whole record—psychedelic, ominous, asking for love amid all the strange sounds and chaotic elements we were making.

Monkeys Uptown

I knew you well, I know you best
A baby mouth
denied the breast
A lazy bone, an eagle eye
Circling a city
that's higher than the sky

And it's looking like you
better do what they say
Those monkeys uptown
who told you not to fuck around
Heaven's a name and the river is brown
With all the mud and the rain
and never settles down

Your baby left you unimpressed
But no one likes a beggar
slightly overdressed
And trouble comes in funky clothes
You can always find
a razor lying in the road

And it's looking like you
better do what they say
Those monkeys uptown
who told you not to fuck around
Heaven's a name and the river is brown
With all the mud and the rain
and never settles down

I knew you well, I know you best
Everybody owes something
to everybody else
Gabriel gave me some news
to give to you
Maybe taking for granted
you'd nothing better to do

And it's looking like you
better do what they say
Those monkeys uptown
who told you not to fuck around
Heaven's a name and the river is brown
With all the mud and the rain
and never settles down

Morning

Hard light
Take the wings off the winter
Song bird
They were strong hands that held her
Miles above ground
We can't see you now

Morning
Took the reins from the rider
Strong hands
On the lap behind her
That tear her nightgown
We can't see you now

Muddy Hymnal

We found your name
across the chapel door
Carved in cursive
with a table fork
Muddy hymnals
And some boot marks where you'd been

The shaking preacher
told the captain's man
The righteous suffer
in a fallen land
And pulled the shade
To keep the crowd
from peeking in

We found your children
by the tavern door
With wooden buttons
and an apple core
Playing house
And telling everyone you'd drowned

The begging choir
told the captain's man
We all assume the worst
the best we can
And for a round or two
They'd gladly track you down

We found you sleeping
by your lover's stone
A ream of paper
and a telephone
A broken bow
Across a long lost violin

Your lover's angel
told the captain's man
It never ends
the way we had it planned
And kissed her palm
And placed it on
your dreaming head

My Lady's House

There is light
in my lady's house
Then there's none
but some falling rain
Less like a spoken word
She is more than
her thousand names

No hands are
half as gentle
Or firm as they'd like to be
Thank God you see me
the way you do
Strange as you are to me

It is good
in my lady's house
Every shape
that her body makes
Love is a fragile word
In the air,
on the length we lay

No hands are
half as gentle
Or firm as they'd like to be
Thank God you see me
the way you do
Strange as you are to me

My Side of the Road

Saw you take it on the chin
outside the Phoenix Motor Inn
You could always find a way
to kill the bird and keep the flame
Somehow lighter on your feet
crossing the dark end of the street
Falling harder than a star
cause you could hear the broken heart

Within the world
But that ain't your song,
you won't sing along

Mission bugs out every night
to throw themselves into the light
Always waking from a dream
of blowing up and burning clean
Saw you cold and getting wet,
sucking the ends of cigarettes
You learned how to love a scar
cause you could hear the broken heart

But you won't sing that sad song
Saw you run and hide, I saw you slide across the sky
But I never saw you down on my side of the road

Saw you take it on the chin
and fix it back with bobby pins
Saw you lose before the start,
I saw you shining in the dark
Saw you change, I saw you choke,
saw you running out of rope
Saw you shaking off the blues,
I saw you recognize the tune

But you won't sing that sad song
San Fran's too much for me to bear,
I thought for sure you'd meet me there
But I never saw you down on my side of the road

Naked as We Came

She says, "Wake up,
it's no use pretending"
I'll keep stealing,
breathing her
Birds are leaving
over autumn's ending
One of us will die
inside these arms
Eyes wide open,
naked as we came
One will spread our ashes
round the yard

She says, "If I leave
before you, darling
Don't you waste me
in the ground"
I lay smiling
like our sleeping children
One of us will die
inside these arms
Eyes wide open,
naked as we came
One will spread our ashes
round the yard

SHE SAYS "WAKE UP,
IT'S NO USE PRETENDING."

I'LL KEEP STEALING,
BREATHING HER

BIRDS ARE LEAVING
OVER
~~QUICKLY~~ AUTUMN'S ENDING

ONE OF US WILL DIE INSIDE THESE ARMS

EYES WIDE OPEN
NAKED AS WE CAME
ONE WILL SPREAD OUR
ASHES AROUND THE YARD

SHE SAYS, "IF ~~I~~ ~~COMING~~

LEAVE BEFORE YOU, DARLING,

PLEASE DON'T WASTE ME

IN THE GROUND"

I LAY SMILING LIKE

THE SLEEPING CHILDREN

ONE OF US WILL DIE INSIDE THESE ARMS

EYES WIDE OPEN

NAKED AS WE CAME

ONE WILL SPREAD OUR

ASHES AROUND THE YARD

New Mexico's
No Breeze

God gave you red light on every green road sign
when you left Santa Fe
We were two string beans and you were too nineteen
to be blowing away
There were thieves in the square hiding hands
and hiding prayers in all their mumbling
Nothing left you alone,
tangled hills and tiny vireo singing something

Stuck with her pin curls,
your mama was scared of the world,
it was born with a bang
I was stepping on sea shells
by the old Mission San Miguel
when a bell tower rang
And the sky fell apart, heard the rain,
I heard your heart, and what was spoken
Was "nothing begs for a name,
nothing wants to stay the same, and nothing's broken"

When your friends and their friends
passed the pipe or tied the knot
Honeymoon music played
in the drive thru parking lot
I woke up by your bed,
you were wandering around the yard
Window wide as the day
but the sun just hit too hard

Little low votive doors,
mama's house slowed a little more every evening
Naked boys throwing stones,
beady eyes and desert bones, they saw you leaving

God gave you bobwhites and the good kind of black night
when you left Santa Fe
New Mexico's no breeze and you were so nineteen,
you were blowing away

Next to Paradise

We take the sun
We take the truth from
anyone, anyone, anyone
We take the wind
Just like the world will
never end, never end, never end

When heaven had enough of us
We turned around and found
forget-me-nots another new surprise
Heaven had enough of us
And no one's knocking on
the nicest houses next to paradise

We take the rain
The pain that comes and goes
again and again and again
Just like a song
We want a place where
we belong, we belong, we belong

We want the devil in the dark woods
'Cause he's calling all our names
Just like the river dragging us all into the sea
We want the leaves against the window
'Cause they don't ever look the same
I want you to tell me
you'll never have enough of me

We take the waves
We take forever to behave,
please behave, please behave
Just like the moon
We take our time and leave too soon,
way too soon, way too soon

'Cause heaven had enough of us
We turned around and found
forget-me-nots another new surprise
Heaven had enough of us
And no one's knocking on
the nicest houses next to paradise

The Night Descending

Black hair, the night descending
Baby never puts her trust in
Tight black tie too quick to laughter
Ain't no telling what he's after

Found a friend without religion
Riding on a stolen engine
Far too fast to pacify you
Ain't no telling what he's up to

In time, the night may soften
Trust that I'm still hoping, darling
Wooden coin, he called my daughter
No good knowing what came after

Met a man with missing fingers
Shaking hands with shaded strangers
Far too strong to pacify you
Ain't no telling what they're up to

Late night, the cock crows shortly
Morning through the open doorway
All us servants beg the master
Ain't no knowing what he's after

In a year of fallen angels
Broken hands and boys in danger
Pray the Lord may pacify you
Ain't no telling what he's up to

No Moon

Black dog bit through the keeper's chain
Small and angry when the devil came
Sold my soul like a pocket knife
There was no moon
There'll be no milk as sweet

Tomcat curled on a rabbit cage
Brittle fingers in the potter's clay
Sold my soul and I laid her down
There was no moon
There'll be no milk as sweet

Bluebird laughs on a fallen tree
Sunset burns on a quiet sea
Sold my soul and they ran me down
There was no moon
There'll be no milk as sweet

On Your Wings

God, there is gold
hidden deep in the ground
God, there's a hangman
that wants to come around

How we rise when we're born
Like the ravens in the corn
On their wings, on our knees
Crawling careless from the sea

God give us love in the time that we have

God, there are guns
growing out of our bones
God, every road
takes us farther from home

All these men that you've made
How we wither in the shade
Of your trees, on your wings
We are carried to the sea

God give us love in the time that we have

Our Light Miles

What will become of us?
Tall trees blown bare
In the bone white snow
Nothing but night for songs
Old mouth still sucking
Warm milk of summer

Love in this breath so long
Thrown against stone
We're hard to get happy
What will become of us?
All water knows leaving
Hearts bleed their changes

Lightning's alive 'cause it disappears
Feel every tear as it falls away

No one looks wrong in rain
Hope builds a house
Too much prayer to tear down
Cloud comes our way so wide
Over the hill
Must be light miles of promise

Pagan Angel and a Borrowed Car

Love was a promise made of smoke
In a frozen copse of trees
A bone cold and older than our bodies
Slowly floating in the sea

Every morning there were planes
The shiny blades of pagan angels in our father's sky
Every evening I would watch her hold the pillow
Tight against her hollows,
Her unholy child

I was still a beggar shaking out my stolen coat
Among the angry cemetery leaves
When they caught the king beneath a borrowed car
Righteous drunk and fumbling for the royal keys

Love was our father's flag
And sewn like a shank in a cake on our leather boots
A beautiful feather floating down
To where the birds had shit our empty chapel pews

Every morning we found one more machine
To mock our ever waning patience at the well
Every evening she'd descend the mountain
Stealing socks and singing something good
Where all their horses fell

Like a snake within the wilted garden wall
I'd hint to her every possibility
While with his gun, the pagan angel rose to say
"My love is one made to break every bended knee"

Passing Afternoon

There are times that walk from you like some passing afternoon
Summer warmed the open window of her honeymoon
And she chose a yard to burn but the ground remembers her
Wooden spoons, her children stir her bougainvillea blooms

There are things that drift away like our endless, numbered days
Autumn blew the quilt right off the perfect bed she made
And she's chosen to believe in the hymns her mother sings
Sunday pulls its children from their piles of fallen leaves

There are sailing ships that pass all our bodies in the grass
Springtime calls her children until she lets them go at last
And she's chosen where to be, though she's lost her wedding ring
Somewhere near her misplaced jar of bougainvillea seeds

There are things we can't recall, blind as night that finds us all
Winter tucks her children in, her fragile china dolls
But my hands remember hers, rolling around the shaded ferns
Naked arms, her secrets still like songs I'd never learned

There are names across the sea, only now I do believe
Sometimes, with the windows closed, she'll sit and think of me
But she'll mend his tattered clothes and they'll kiss as if they know
A baby sleeps in all our bones, so scared to be alone

Peace Beneath the City

Here's a prayer for the body
buried by the interstate
Mother of a soldier,
a tree in a forest up in flames
Black valley, peace beneath the city
Where the women hear the washboard rhythm
in their bosom when they say
"Give me good legs
and a Japanese car and show me a road"

Sing a song for the bodies
buried by the riverbank
A well-dressed boy and a pig
with a bullet in the brain
Black valley, peace beneath the city
Where the white girls wander
the strip mall, singing all day
"Give me a juggernaut heart
and a Japanese car and someone to free"

Say something for the body
buried like a keepsake
Mother of a million mouths
with the very same name
Black valley, peace beneath the city
Where the women tell the weather
but never ever tell you what they pray
They pray, "Give me a yellow brick road
and a Japanese car and benevolent change"

Postcard

This postcard tells you where we've been
And dirty dreams of pious men
Who wake in fear but sleep again
With what they've done
With what they've done
With all they've done

Some prophet died but wrote it down
Our serpent bellies on the ground
And all the ladies singing loud
"Hallelujah"
"Hallelujah"
"Hallelujah"

The meadow birds have found the bones
Of righteous men like ragged clothes
Like precious stones
And fell like evil in the end
And ate of them, those evil men
Those perfect men

Some knuckle broken on disease
Which pulled a preacher off his knees
A callous whisper through the trees
Blows, "Patience, boy"
"More patience, boy"
"More patience, boy"

And watch your children by the flame
The ones you gave your father's name
Whose evil and his love remain
Inside you, boy
Inside you, boy
Inside you, boy

The meadow birds have found the bones
Of righteous men like ragged clothes
Like precious stones
And fell like evil in the end
And ate of them, those evil men
Those perfect men

We'll sing a song we've never heard
Formed out of small forsaken words
And all the while that this occurs
We'll love you all
We'll love you all
We'll love you all

And for the beauty that we've lost
The measured time for love it cost
Despite our feelings for the cross
We love you all
We love you all
We love you all

Prison on Route 41

There's a prison on route 41
A home to my father, first cousin, and son
and I visit on every weekend
Not with my body
But with prayers that I send

I've a reason for my absentee
And no lack of love for my dear family
But my savior is not Christ the Lord
But one named Virginia
Whom I live my life for

'Cause I owe mine to her
And I'd rot in that prison for sure
If she'd tossed me aside
And not shown me the way to abide

By the creed, the law of the land
Unlike my uncle, grandpa, and great aunt
Whom I'd most likely see every day
If not for the righteous path
Virginia's laid

There's a prison on route 41
A home to my mother, step-brother, and son
And I'd tear down that jail by myself
if not for Virginia
Who made me someone else

And I owe all to her
And I'd rot in that prison for sure
If she'd tossed me aside
And not shown me the way to abide

By the precepts of her purity
So unlike the habits of my whole family
Who I only see down on my knees
In prayer by Virginia
Whom I live for to please

Promise What You Will

Lately she don't care
For a warmer breeze
Or shade around the base
Of the maple trees
Spring was on the mountain
We climbed upon
Stopped to see how high
And how far we'd gone

I said, "Love is waiting
And better days"
She smiled and placed a kiss
On my waiting face
"Promise what you will
Something good for me
Time will take it all
And it will, you'll see"

Promising Light

Time and all you gave
I was the jerk who preferred the sea
To tussling in the waves
Tugging your skirt, singing please, please, please

But now I see love
Tracked on the floor where you walked outside
Now I see love
Looking for you in this other girl's eyes

Time and all you took
Only my freedom to fuck the whole world
Promising not to look
Promising light on the sidewalk girls

But now I see love
There in your car where I said those things
Now I see love
Tugging your skirt, singing please, please, please

Time and all you gave
There on your cross that I never saw
Well beyond the waves
Dunking my head when I heard you call

But now I see love
There in the scab where you pinched my leg
Now I see love
There on your side of my empty bed

Quarters in a Pocket

Like the setting sun
And more than anyone
You look warmer when you're sinking down

Find your favorite tree
And come sit next to me
I've a sheet that's softer than the ground

'Cause time spent with you
Feels like charcoal sketches for a painting
That you won't let me see
But I've come to find
Comfort comes like quarters in a pocket
I thought were lost to me

All your favorite clothes
And all the pain you know
Came from those you favored for a time

Take it off your chest
And throw your loneliness
In a surly river, cold and wild

'Cause time spent with you
Feels like charcoal sketches for a painting
That you won't let me see
But I've come to find
Comfort comes like quarters in a pocket
I thought were lost to me

Lie about your sign
And hang your worry lines
On a missing poster for a dog

Find a promise ring
And blind affinity
For a match the gypsy said was wrong

'Cause time spent with you
Feels like charcoal sketches for a painting
That you won't let me see
But I've come to find
Comfort comes like quarters in a pocket
Discovered accidentally

Rabbit Will Run

The last I saw mother,
she rose from her chair
When they caught me,
I'd just finished combing my hair
'Cause a rabbit will run
and the colt hasn't long with the mare
We've all learned the earth
while we carried the throne
We dove under the rivers
and under our clothes
And I still have a prayer,
as sure as my settling bones

The last I saw mother,
she covered my ears
When they caught me,
I offered the captain a beer
'Cause a rabbit will run,
and the lion has nothing to fear
We've bricked up the garden
and know what it means
And we've all kissed the virgin
as if she were clean
And I still have a prayer
despite all the colors I've seen

And judgement is just like
a cup that we share
I'll jump over the wall
and I'll wait for you there
Well past the weeds
in our vision of things to come
We've all heard the rooster
and all been denied
And we've seen through the haze
and the spit in our eyes
And I still have a prayer,
a well-weathered word to the wise

The last I saw mother,
she smelled like a rose
When they caught me,
the captain, he opened my nose

'Cause a rabbit will run
and the wind takes a bird where it blows
We've all traded lovers
and woke up alone
And we've clapped for the king
though our fingers were cold
And I still have a prayer
because I love what I cannot control

The last I saw mother,
she acted surprised
When they caught me,
the captain, he cried like a child
'Cause a rabbit will run
and good dogs together go wild
We've all envied grace
at the end of the day
And we've armed all the children
we thought we betrayed
And I still have a prayer,
though too few occasions to pray

And judgement is just like
a cup that we share
I'll jump over the wall
and I'll wait for you there
Well past the weeds
in our vision of things to come
We've all found a reason
for hiding the gun
And we've helped out a few
if we've hurt anyone
And I still have a prayer and so be it,
I've done what I've done

The last I saw mother,
she blew me a kiss
When they caught me,
the cuffs cut the blood from my wrists
'Cause a rabbit will run
and a pig has to lay in its piss
We've all given half
to the hand in our face
We've all taken a stone
from the holiest place
And I still have a prayer
and I've furthered the world in my way

Radio War

Did the wine make her dream
Of the far distant spring
Or a bed full of hens
Or the ghost of a friend

All the while that she wept
She'd a gun by her bed
And a letter he wrote
From a dry, foundered boat

And the train track will take
All the wounded ones home
And I'll be alone
Fare thee well, Sara Jones

Now we lie on the floor
While the radio war
Finds its way through the air
Of the dead market square

And the beast never seen
Licks its red talons clean
Sara curses the cold
"No more snow, no more snow"

Red Dust

Dusk is red
and red dust plays
On the wind
nears Daniel's place
Danny's sick
and smaller boy
Rhythm lingers on and on
On and on

Dusk is dead
the sun gone down
Danny's boy
lies in the ground
Guitar on the
dead boy's chest
The devil's granted
last request
Plays on and on
On and on

Resurrection Fern

In our days, we will live like our ghosts will live
Pitching glass at the cornfield crows and folding clothes
Like stubborn boys across the road, we'll keep everything
Grandma's gun and the black bear claw that took her dog

And when Sister Lowery says, "Amen," we won't hear anything
The ten-car train will take that word, that fledgling bird
And the fallen house across the way, it'll keep everything
The baby's breath, our bravery wasted and our shame

And we'll undress beside the ashes of the fire
Both our tender bellies wound in baling wire
All the more a pair of underwater pearls
Than the oak tree and its resurrection fern

In our days, we will say what our ghosts will say
"We gave the world what it saw fit and what'd we get"
Like stubborn boys with big green eyes, we'll see everything
In the timid shade of the autumn leaves and the buzzard's wing

And we'll undress beside the ashes of the fire
Our tender bellies wound around in baling wire
All the more, a pair of underwater pearls
Than the oak tree and its resurrection fern

Right for Sky

Know this house that I called home
Her gentle milk was happy just to flow
Know that her tomcats took their licks in turn
Some branches fall to open arms
Some paradises are a prayer too far
God's in the treetop making mockingbirds

If I could choose I would do things right
Teach my dreams to look me in the eye
Sing my heart out into my hand
Shine where light demands

When I lose my feet in my father's shoes
When I take your flesh with my false tooth
When I bend until I break in two
Call me a fool being green
In the leaves of the world

The wind blows all the wild away
This house was kind as every hiding place
Bones are the hardest offering to burn
That dog will bark though no one's there
This man went mad breaking his easy chair
Sing me the softest heart I've ever heard

It's only right how this trail goes cold
Moonlight gliding through our empty clothes
Know I'm warm when a cloud rolls by
Rolling right for sky

When I lose my feet in my father's shoes
When I take your flesh with my false tooth
When I bend until I break in two
Call me a fool being green
In the leaves of the world

KNOW THIS HOUSE THAT I CALLED HOME
HER GENTLE MILK WAS HAPPY JUST TO FLOW
KNOW THAT HER TOMCATS TOOK THEIR LICKS IN TURN
SOME BRANCHES FALL TO OPEN ARMS
SOME PARADISES ARE A PRAYER TOO FAR
GODS IN THE TREETOP MAKING MOCKINGBIRDS
IF I MAKE TROUBLE, I'LL MAKE IT RIGHT
~~MAKE~~ MY DREAM TO LOOK ME IN THE EYE
~~SO~~ SING MY HEART OUT INTO MY HAND
SHINE WHERE LIGHT DEMANDS
WHEN I LOSE MY FEET IN MY FATHER'S SHOES
WHEN I TAKE YOUR FLESH WITH MY FALSE TOOTH
WHEN I BEND UNTIL I BREAK IN TWO
JUST CALL ME A FOOL BEING GREEN
IN THE LEAVES OF THE WORLD
THE WIND BLOWS ALL THE WILD AWAY
THIS HOUSE WAS KIND AS ANY HIDING PLACE
HER BONES WERE THE HARDEST OFFERING TO BURN
~~SOME DO~~
                            THOUGH
THAT DOG WILL BARK ~~WHEN~~ NO ONE'S THERE
THAT MAN WENT MAD BREAKING HIS EASY CHAIR
SING ME THE SOFTEST HEART I'VE EVER HEARD
~~FAR BEHIND~~ FAR BEHIND ME MY TRACKS ARE COLD
~~IF YOU LOSE ME MY TRAIL GOES COLD~~
MOONLIGHT GLIDING THROUGH MY EMPTY CLOTHES
KNOW I'M WARM AS A CLOUD ROLLS BY
LOST INSIDE THE SKY

The Rooster Moans

Crack of dawn, the rooster moans
Wake up boy, you're far from home
Serpentine, the tracks in flames
Longest path the devil laid
Led you straight aboard this rusty train

Lift your head because you can't sleep
Bite your lip because you can't eat
Darkest den the devil made
Jesus weeps but he's been paid
Not to ride inside this rusty train

Buzzard's breath, the rooster moans
Stow it boy, you're far from home
Stow your sorrow, stow your fear
What did you do to end up here?
End up on the devil's rusty train

Sacred Vision

There's no way to temper your thirst
With lasting impressions or pictures of home
"There's no way to grow that don't hurt"
She growled from the station then hung up the phone

There's no sacred vision like her
No eye crushing mountain or jewelry to wear
There's no granted wish I'd prefer
Then she to be with me or us to be there

I'd rather to be all alone
Forgiveness is fickle when trust is a chore
"It's not every sin that's atoned"
I heard her speak softly then heard her no more

There's no sacred vision like her
No eye crushing mountain or jewelry to wear
There's no granted wish I'd prefer
Than she to be with me or us to be there

The Sea and the Rhythm

Tonight, we're the sea and the salty breeze
the milk from your breast is on my lips
and lovelier words from your mouth to me
when salty my sweat and fingertips

Our hands they seek the end of afternoon
My hands believe and move over you

Tonight, we're the sea and the rhythm there
the waves and the wind and night is black
tonight we're the scent of your long black hair
spread out like your breath across my back

Your hands they move like waves over me
beneath the moon, tonight, we're the sea

Serpent Charmer

There's a woman hater
with a broken record player
And a dusty compass out to map
the country's new behavior
Strange words and we all roll back
into the river
With brave boys
in the empty coats of men

There's a kitchen timer,
distractions and reminders
Like a roly-poly slowly crawling
across your family china
Strange words and we all roll back
into the river
Where dead dogs
only want to live again

There's a serpent charmer
with a pair of shoes in water
And a speeding ticket you got
leading that last lamb to slaughter
Strange words and we all roll back
into the river
Where good girls come
and kick you in the shin

There's a hopeful hunter
with a hapless sense of wonder
And a million claw marks
on the rock he hid his money under
Strange words and we all roll back
into the river
And made men only
want to live again

Show Him the Ground

Did the fighting begin
With a knock on your chin
With the dirt on your clothes
Or the blood from your nose?

Did you curse his name
And the women that gave him the same?
Would it make you feel much better
To show him the ground?

Do you think you'd be weak
If you both turned a cheek?
There's a cloud in the sky
That blocks the sun from your eyes

If you curse his name
And the women that gave him the same
Would you feel big and strong
The next time that they come around?

Sing Song Bird

Give me your shoulder, I'm a sing song bird
My savior says that I've the words
A map across the daylight blinding you
Chicken-boned and with a ten cent bunk
When Jesus spoke, though I was drunk
He tied my shoe and told me what to do

Warn the boys about the dimmer rooms
Who try to woo them all with their cheap perfume
Moonlight clears a pathway to the fall
Warn the girls about the dimmer stars
Who try to woo them all with their cheap guitars
The morning fades glitter on us all

Warn the boys about the dimmer rooms
Who try to woo them all with their cheap perfume
The sun don't sweat the souls that get the call
Warn the girls about the dimmer stars
Who try to woo them all with their cheap guitars
Dear Lord, give me the strength to shade you all

Ghost on Ghost

I went to New York and played with some jazz guys! I'd had horns on tour for *Kiss Each Other Clean*—my friends Elliot Bergman and Stuart Bogie—and they sounded so great I knew I wanted to explore those sounds some more. I also wanted to try using strings, another thing that I hadn't really ever fooled with. I wanted these different elements, but not as an afterthought. I wanted to start there. So I asked Rob Burger to help me do the arrangements, make a map for the players to follow. He did a great job leading the ship.

The band was incredible. Brian Blade was a revelation—just natural and loose and expressive, one of the most incredible drummers I've ever played with. Hopefully in some next life I'll be a drummer. I just love being in the middle of the rhythm section. Tony Garnier was on the bass. He plays with Dylan and was in Asleep at the Wheel and the Lounge Lizards. What a résumé. I asked him what Dylan's like, and he said, "I could tell you, but I'd have to kill *myself*."

We had some great horn players, so we ended up doing a version of "Lovers' Revolution" in the style of some of Charles Mingus's music from the fifties. It was incredible. I just gave them the nudge and they would run with it. Some amazing solos, even shouting together from the bandstand! To this day, I can't believe some of the talent in the room that day. Doug Wieselman, he was killing me! Curtis Fowlkes, Tony Scherr, Kenny Wollesen . . . lots of really inspiring players.

I felt lucky and blessed to be able to do that, but I also felt ready. If someone had told me when I was making *Endless Numbered Days* that that was going to happen, I'd probably have peed in my pants from nervousness. But by this point I felt like I was ready.

I remember having to earn these songs. I'd been so busy. We'd built a new house and studio in Texas, moved, and our fifth child had been born. I remember being really distracted and kind of losing my mind. The work just felt different. I really had to drag these songs up the hill.

If you listen across my records, you'll often find recurring images. I find that I end up doing that a lot. There's something that catches my imagination over the course of a year or so, and it ends up appearing in different songs—usually unintentionally, to be honest. But when you hear them all together, it feels like a motif. It's serendipitous and really fun.

When the record came out, I said in an interview that it told the story of one couple's cross-country journey. That was total bullshit. I didn't have a throughline for what the record was about. I never do. In hindsight, I recognized a pattern where a lot of the songs had a couple in them, but what song about a romantic situation doesn't?

I was also into place names. When you mention a city, it comes with all the baggage and narrative and history of that city. You insert it into your song without actually having to describe much. It's similar to the way I was using names from the Bible. I ended up using so many place names that the whole thing felt a little like a couple's journey through these towns, or a snapshot of different couples in different towns. And so I enshrined them on the cover in a gold frame, with a photograph by Barbara Crane. I thought it was beautiful, and punk rock in its own way. I felt like I knew who those young people were—just starting their journey, for better or worse.

What ties this group of songs together more than anything, I think, is the songwriting technique. Generally, I don't write autobiographical songs, but there are usually autobiographical elements. After all, you only have one life to draw your experience from. But this one has even less of that. Instead, I was trying a slightly different poetic style. Where the previous two records borrowed a lot from the Beats, these drew more from the confessional poets. It's less political and more personal. The phrase "ghost on ghost" in "Grace for Saints and Ramblers" is from James Wright, a poem called "What the Earth Asked Me":

> "What good will pity do the lost
> Who flutter in the driven wind,
> Wild for the body, ghost on ghost?"
>   No good, no good to me.

I read a lot of poetry, and while I don't necessarily look to other people to tell me what to write, I love seeing different ways to communicate. The way we use language can be so surprising and provocative. Different perspectives, too. Unique ways of seeing. When I read a great poem, I get the urge to immediately find a pen and paper. It gets me going, reading pieces that engage with the language that way. Honestly, I feel like *Our Endless Numbered Days* wouldn't exist the way that it does without Mary Oliver. Her recognition of sacred natural space and our place in it informed a lot of my thinking then.

I was absorbing stuff that was also very affecting—Wright, Richard Hugo, Philip Levine, Carolyn Forché—and taught me about the potential for language and what kind of subjects to draw from that I might not have expected before. I think maybe I was getting bored of my own imagery—the dark, beautiful but sort of chaotic images. Instead, I was interested in the personal landscape, the travel experience, and these poets gave me a rejuvenated sense of the joy of language.

There's a lot of playfulness, too. An open approach that I now prefer. I feel like I was more successful at it with this one. If you read "The Desert Babbler" out loud, I hope it holds up as a poem, a portrait of two people and a place. I also like when the songs start to feel like they're having a conversation with themselves and each other. And when the frame of the picture keeps widening in unexpected ways. All of those interests together painted this record.

I feel like people kind of tuned out to this one. I think they decided I'd betrayed my roots and I was never coming back. Me, I was just following the muse, and I think it's a great record. I pushed myself as far as I could go toward this sort of sophisticated blues/jazz/rock/folk thing, trying to blend these different musical styles and traditions and spit them out as something that I could call my own. But it felt like it was the end of a journey. After this, we moved away from Texas, and it was time to reset everything.

Singers and the Endless Song

When we all ran back into the briars
We told our children about the foreign shore
When we threw our boots into the fire
We told them all about the tug of war
Gonna tell them about the seed and the shovel
About the prison and the promised land
Gonna tell them about the dream of the devil
About the hurting and the healing hand

When we held our words up in the mirror
We told our children how to hold their tongues
When we held our heads beneath the river
We told them all about the iron lung
Gonna tell them about the sins of the father
About the junkie and the jubilee
Gonna tell them about the roots in the water
About the killing in the quiet line of trees

All our morning kisses in the covers
They told our children what "worthy" means
And then you wrapped your arms around another
And told them what was worth a pile of beans
Gonna tell them about the call of the ocean
About the singers and the endless song
Gonna tell them about the body and the motion
And how the music never lasts too long

About the low lit alley and the wedding bed
About the first born sucker and the spider's web
About the mind and the muscle and the weary mile
About the heart and the hustle and the empty sky
About the tangled up truth in the perfect teeth
About the pilgrim and the picking through the chaff and wheat
About the breeze in the summer and the nose will know
About the sleep through the winter when the cold wind blows
About the lame duck lion and a thorny crown
About the proud punk mule and the heavy plow
About the butterfly kiss and the call for blood
About the pig and the preacher and the holy mud
About the sunburned belly and the mother's moon
About the end of the music coming way too soon

Sinning Hands

Midnight, and her eyes hide like kittens, new and wet
Mine are sinning hands on her, lying on my bed

The river still may rise, wild and water take us both
Mine are sinning hands, take our bodies, take our clothes

Bloodless moonlight, may my lady
Give her lovely skin and bones

Midnight, and my bride treads in distant water now
Mine are sinning hands and my teeth have fallen out

The river still may rise, though it took more than it gave
Mine are sinning hands on a broken windowpane

Bloodless moonlight, like my lady
Gave me only skin and bones

Sixteen, Maybe Less

Beyond the ridge to the left,
you asked me what I want
Between the trees and cicadas
singing around the pond
"I've spent an hour with you,
should I want anything else"

One grinning wink,
like the neon on a liquor store
We were sixteen,
maybe less, maybe a little more
I walked home smiling,
I finally had a story to tell

And though an autumn time lullaby
Sang our newborn love to sleep
My brother told me he saw you there
In the woods one Christmas Eve, waiting

I met my wife at a party
when I drank too much
My son is married
and tells me we don't talk enough
Call it predictable,
yesterday my dream was of you

Beyond the ridge to the west,
the sun had left the sky
Between the trees and pond,
you put your hand in mine
Said, "Time has bridled us both
but I remember you too"

And though an autumn time lullaby
Sang our newborn love to sleep
I dreamt I traveled and found you there
In the woods one Christmas Eve waiting

Slow Black River

Lost my watch, watch, and chain
But time's not lost
This time we walk together
Beside the slow black river

Water-walking over mud
You whisper something
Something good in my ear
So I stop so I can hear

Darling, I'm the one to blame
I threw your watch and chain to where I don't know
Inside the tall grass meadow

You'll forget, forget in time
Remember this
Your hand in mine forever
Beside the slow black river

Lost my watch, watch, and chain
To her today
But time, it has no meaning
When her and me are walking

Darling, I'm the one to blame
I love you still
And timeless now forever
Together by the river

Sodom, South Georgia

Papa died smiling
Wide as the ring of a bell
Gone all-star white
Small as a wish in a well
And Sodom, South Georgia
Woke like a tree full of bees
Buried in Christmas
Bows and a blanket of weeds

Papa died Sunday
and I understood
All dead white boys say,
"God is good"
White tongues hang out,
"God is good"

Papa died while my
Girl lady Edith was born
Both heads fell like
Eyes on a crack in the door
And Sodom, South Georgia
Slept on an acre of bones
Slept through Christmas
Slept like a bucket of snow

Papa died Sunday
and I understood
All dead white boys say,
"God is good"
White tongues hang out,
"God is good"

Someday the Waves

Waking before you
I've got a fever
and a childish wish for snow
Seems like a long, long time
Since I spun you
to this borrowed radio

You pick a place
that's where I'll be
time, like your cheek
has turned for me

Someday the waves will stop
every aching
old machine will feel no pain
someday we both will walk
Where a baby
made tomorrow is again

Waking before you
I'm like the lord
who sees his love though we don't know
seems like a long, long time
since I've been above you
seen and loved you so

You pick a place
that's where I'll be
time, like your cheek
has turned for me

Song in Stone

Songbirds in the morning had my head
Lost in the tall trees I knew well
Well I would say
Dreaming my dry weeds
Stray life finds its way to all of us
Say something green it comes back sun
Light on my lips
Let them kiss dark leaves

Let the hands of the wrong prophets
Heal me all they should
Let the wine of the poison jesuses taste good

When all those trees lay down
If you were a bird and fell into my arms
If I wrote your song in stone
If I wore your wings back home
Would the dreams in the backwater
Drown us far from harm

Give this to the gray it comes back gold
Birds of the morning they may know
No more than us
Giving their hymns for life

Let the waves on the wrong water
Say what they will say
While the wind in the broken branches
Blows me away

All tall trees lay down
If you were the bird who fell into my arms
I could write your song in stone
I could wear your wings back home
Where the dreams in the backwater
Drown us far from harm

Southern Anthem

Just like the way that you ran to wine
When they made the new milk turn
Jesus, a friend in the better times
Let your mother's Bible burn
Freedom, a fever you suffered through
And the dog drank from your cup
Frozen, the river that baptized you
And the horse died standing up

But when a southern anthem rings
She will buckle to that sound
When that southern anthem sings
It will lay her burdens down

Just like the way that you lost your guns
When they cut the clothesline loose
Jesus, a friend of the weaker ones
Said, "I'm all they stole from you"
Freedom, a thistle that withered dry
Still a baby in your hands
Frozen, the ground refused to die
And the guitar rose again

And when that southern anthem rings
She will buckle to the sound
When that southern anthem sings
It will lay her burdens down

Straight and Tall

Don't tell me all the shit you've done
How you push your luck with everyone
'Cause your mean upbringing left you a mess

Don't tell me all the shit you'd say
If some fool jerked you around thataway
You ain't done half of what you confess

That ain't you, as far as I can tell
That ain't you, although you wear it well
That ain't you, after all
You're just standing up, laying down, straight and tall

Don't tell me that you understand
How to brave the world and be a man
Unless you must convince yourself

Don't tell me I should be like you
I should learn from what you say and do
Don't ask the poor to share the wealth

That ain't you, as far as I can tell
That ain't you, although you wear it well
That ain't you, after all
You're just standing up, laying down, straight and tall

Stranger Lay Beside Me

I was bad, I was good, running wild through the woods
While the branches above me were burning
I was breathing the smoke, I was starting to choke
When a stranger lay beside me

I was lost, I was found, you were hanging around
Moving slowly but headed for glory
I was healed, I was hurt, I was sinning in church
When a stranger lay beside me

I was snuffed, I was stoked, there was love in us both
And a buzzard was circling the valley
I was chaff, I was wheat, I was bone, I was meat
When a stranger lay beside me

I was close, I was far, feral cats in the car
And a crack in the roof that kept dripping
I was numb when I smiled, I was built and defiled
When a stranger lay beside me

And the moon rose again and the snake shed its skin
Every hand in the city was shaking
We were kissed, we were clawed, given just to be robbed
We needed the love we were making

I was present and gone, said "farewell" and "so long"
Then came back 'cause the street was too empty
I was nursing a bruise, thought for sure it was you
When a stranger lay beside me

I was strong, I was weak, all the hens were asleep
And the hawk's only kind 'cause he's hungry
I was sold, I was bought, I was promised a lot
When a stranger lay beside me

I was wrong, I was right, you were poised in the light
Both as evil as ever and holy
I was bitten and chewed, bound and gagged on the truth
When a stranger lay beside me

I was soft, I was hard, the sky heavy with stars
Never meant to surrender their meaning
I was love, I was hate, stuffed and licking my plate
When a stranger lay beside me

I was chided and cheered, we were reeking with fear
That the world might return for its mercy
I was mended and torn, I was killed and reborn
When a stranger lay beside me

And the moon rose again and the snake shed its skin
And the back of the city was breaking
We both took to it well, blind and feeling ourselves
We needed the love we were making

I was captured and freed, the sun set through the trees
And time beat on the length of my body
I was taught, I was teased in the nature of things
When a stranger lay beside me

Beast Epic / Weed Garden

We left Texas and moved to North Carolina. It felt like everything was changing, including what I was looking for in the music.

Being back home, I spent some time with Ben Bridwell and his brother and friends, and that grew into the covers record *Sing into My Mouth*. It was a great way to experiment without the pressure of a regular Iron & Wine record. I was just messing around with friends and having fun.

Our version of the Talking Heads tune "This Must Be the Place" had this sparse, percolating, acoustic sound that pointed me in a new direction. And we did El Perro del Mar's "God Knows (You Gotta Give to Get)." It was this gutted, Big Star, Velvet Underground kind of thing. It felt empty, but with a lot of feedback and strange noise. Those were sounds I wanted to try, and when I did, they felt good. I wanted to keep doing them.

I also did a record with Jesca Hoop, *Love Letter for Fire*. I'd always loved the duet format. I was excited to try my hand at it. Co-writing was a struggle at first, but it became something I really enjoyed. The success was in the casting. In one sense, they were just love-song duets, but we were both interested in approaching the songs a little off-kilter. "Our memories are Christ and our hearts are clothes"— a line from the song "Valley Clouds"—that's not normal language. The words are simple, not fancy, but they're also poetic and expressive in the way the language is used to describe a feeling. Some were playful and intimate-sounding like that, and some were more direct.

Both of those records felt like trying new things—more intimate, more immediate, and more passionate—which is always good in art. I took those two experiences into *Beast Epic*. It was kind of a reset. I took everything I learned from playing with all the jazz musicians from *Ghost on Ghost* and made tunes that were quiet but had a lot of space for different things to happen musically. My idea was to make a record like Van Morrison's *Astral Weeks*, where you feel the folk chord changes but the musicians are playing a lot of other things around them.

We went to the Loft, Wilco's studio in Chicago, with the house engineer Tom Schick recording. I'd become addicted to playing everything live. Some songs require more overdubs than others, but if you create the basis of the track as a live thing, it pushes and pulls with intensity and tempo. Because it's just one big room, the Wilco Loft makes everyone focus on what's happening. There aren't people out in the lounge smoking cigarettes or eating chips. Everyone's in there thinking about what you're making, which is really great.

The players included Teddy Rankin Parker. He'd been in the string section on the *Ghost on Ghost* tour and on the Hoop record. I loved the way he played, so I brought him into this session as well. Sebastian Steinberg was on bass. He plays emotions, not just riffs, and it's very expressive. My songs are pretty sedate, so I feel like they benefit from people being adventurous, and his approach is infectious. We all start thinking about how we can take a few simple chord changes and make it a more dynamic and complicated thing.

We did at least two recording sessions. For the most part, we got everything from the first one, but after mixing we went back to tweak things. Usually I'm just looking for some kind of variety. If there's something missing in the sequencing, we'll go back and do that kind of tune.

A lot of these songs were born rather quickly during or just after the time I was writing with Hoop. That collaboration was the impetus for a new engagement with songwriting. I felt like someone trying to return to their roots, but someone who'd been on a very long journey. Plus, I was going through big changes, and I felt shook up. I'd moved back to the southeast from Texas and was struggling with that. I'd also turned forty, and my body was letting me know who was boss. Basically, it was a midlife crisis. All these songs reflect that sense of things breaking down.

Even a tune like "Call It Dreaming," which has a positive sheen on it, that's kind of a mirage. "Say it's here where our pieces fall in place." Meaning, let's say it's here that everything works out right, that everything is good, even though we know it isn't. You could take that as sincere, sarcastic, or both at the same time.

I think most people have a love-hate relationship with the town they're from, and when we moved back, I felt stifled. "Thomas County Law" was born from a sense that I had walked into a wall. Things I felt I had escaped were coming back to me. It was like crawling back up the birth canal. Not good for anybody involved.

Luckily, as a songwriter, no matter how weird of a spot you're in, you can always channel that into your creative energy and repurpose it. Once I came up with the opening line—"Thomas County law's got a crooked tooth"—I felt like I could go anywhere with that. It's so fun when you get a line like that. It's like you've been given this open premise that you can wander around in.

There's a line in "Bitter Truth" that I'd heard and saved to use in a song. I was at South by Southwest doing an interview along with Ray Wylie Hubbard and Jerry Jeff Walker. At one point, Jerry was talking about a tune he'd done, and he described it as a "getting-even-in-a-song kind of song." I knew exactly what he was talking about. When you're writing, you can say anything you want, 'cause no one's there to talk back to you! So I just tucked that in my pocket.

All these songs were ways of saying, "Man, I feel really broken, and I feel like everyone I know does, too." I wasn't pretending like I had any advice. It just felt like the most honest thing I could sing about at the time. There were quite a few misfit songs, orphans that didn't make it onto the record, since I tend to like shorter albums. We went back to Chicago for a day or two and did a few more tunes for variety's sake. I put the ones that survived the chopping block on an EP and called it *Weed Garden*.

Summer Clouds

Summer clouds blowing
up and down the stairs
By the end we'll take music
from them both
And give it back
shining broken glass

Wet and cold,
I was waiting there for you
You raised your glass
and the scars fell off my heart
We threw a stone
but we never heard it land
There are clouds
keeping quiet every night

By the end we hold something
too high to ever come back down
By the end there's a song we will sing
meant for someone else
By the end we leave somewhere
too long to ever wander back
By the end we give someone
too much to ever close the hand

Summer clouds doing good
for going gray
Tell me where all this love
fits in the world
You can lie,
give me all the rain you want

Summer in Savannah

Summer in Savannah slows a jack rabbit down
But I'm in your car and driving to town
Mama's missing finger had a mind of its own
And the dog that we lost keeps coming home
I'm a ham fist hanging around a soda machine
And the birds don't move in the live oak trees
Pounding on the table, papa said I would learn
That you take what you get and you give what you earn
And then he said you reap just what you sow
So I'm going to take my white house and paint it gold

Summer in Savannah where the breeze never blows
But you're laid on my lap and wearing my clothes
Mama told me lately she was praying for you
So don't hit me just 'cause you're the best I can do
I'm a no neck cursing at a color TV
And the gaslight swirls with June bug wings
Staring at the ceiling, papa struggled to say
You'll find it's all such a drag, but don't get carried away
Because someone said you reap just what you sow
So I'm going to take my white house and paint it gold

Summer in Savannah takes a measure of faith
But I'm under the bed and you're kissing my face
When mama told the cop that I was born in the caul
She meant in the shade and free from the law
And I'm a slack jaw leaning on a newspaper stand
And papa bought a bullet about as big as my hand
We trapped a little hornet in a teacup for fun
And we cut off its head and we still got stung
I think that Jesus said you reap just what you sow
So I'm going to take my white house and paint it gold

Sundown
(Back in the Briars)

There go the cops
with the tomcat teeth
Here come the church
mice trying too hard
She had a way
to be kind with words
I had a knife
in the back of my car

Nobody knows when
the rain may come
Nobody wants to wake up and be cruel
She locked the door
and the sun went down
On South Carolina
with nothing to lose

All of her naked boys
And not even I was true

Sunset Soon Forgotten

Be this sunset soon forgotten
Your brothers left here shaved and crazy
We've learned to hide our bottles in the well
And what's worth keeping, sun still sinking
Down and down
Once again
Down and down
Gone again

Be this sunset one for keeping
This June bug street sings low and lovely
Those band-aid children chased your dog away
She runs, returning, sun still sinking
Down and down
Once again
Down and down
Gone again

Swans and the Swimming

"Take me again,"
she said, thinking of him
"To the pond
with the swans and the swimming"
Far from his room,
that familiar perfume
How it left her
aware she was naked

The lesson she learned
when her memory serves
Is to marvel with
love at the sunset
And walking away,
it's the dark end of day
She will measure
and break like a habit

But oh how the rain sounds
as loud as a lover's words
And now and again,
she's afraid when the sun returns

"Take me again,"
she said, thinking of him
"I don't care for this careful behavior"
A brush through her hair,
children kissing upstairs
Keeps her up
with her want for a savior

The sun on the sand,
on her knees and her hands
As she begs for a fish
from the water
But turns them away,
she's the whip and the slave
Given time she may find
something better

But oh how the rain sounds
as loud as a lover's words
And now and again,
she's afraid when the sun returns

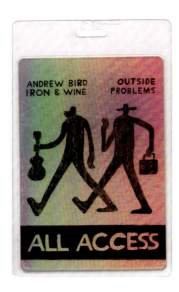
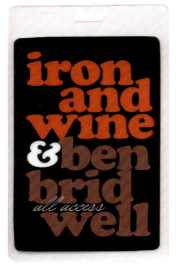
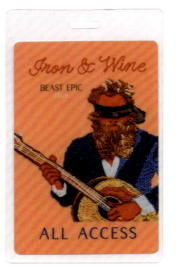
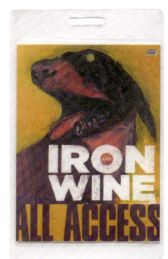

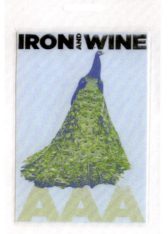
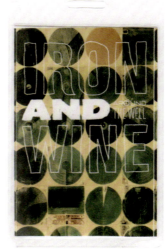

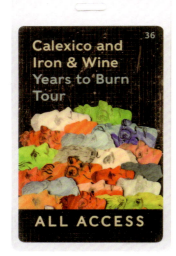
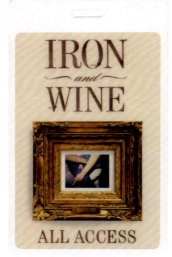

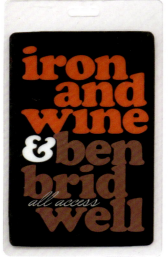

Sweet Talk

Who's here, let's dance
Let's play right into the hands
Of a wonderful life

Let's swing, let's miss
Kiss a little harder on the lips
Of a wonderful life
Go with the flow
Bleed like color on the clothes
Of a wonderful life

Lose another new year
Make it matter
and cry a couple real tears
We could visit
'til we wouldn't want to live here

Sweet talk, let's share
Let's get tangled in the hair
Of a wonderful life
Stick and poke, sit and spin
Let's get underneath the skin
Of a wonderful life

It's only trouble brewing
We'll break even and hide among the ruins
Sounds easy if you've never tried to do it

Let's bow, bow and scrape
Sucker punching straight into the face
Of a wonderful life
Who's there, who knows
Let's leave nothing on the bones
Of a wonderful life

Feel it moving faster
We'll have a cow
and then we'll put it out to pasture
Pray the moment
doesn't take a life to master

Taken by Surprise

I knew someone long ago
She wasn't there and then she was
That lightning hit the ground
without a warning
She would laugh and I would laugh
Somehow that sound became a day
Day turned into night
and night to morning

If she ever comes back around
for something she forgot
Or maybe take me for a ride
I don't get taken by surprise anymore

I knew someone long ago
Although it feels like yesterday
She would look me in the eye and say whatever
I know this kind of moon
It looks too full to come back down
And I've seen a couple suns that set forever

If she ever comes back around
Just to slam an open door
Or to lay her hand in mine
I don't get taken by surprise anymore

I knew someone long ago
Whether I wanted to or not
We never said goodbye that I remember
She never knew how much she gave
How much she made and left behind
I never knew how much I had to surrender

If she ever comes back around
To see if I'm still sore
Or just make me feel alive
I don't get taken by surprise anymore

Talking to Fog

This is our surrender
To the garden, to the weeds
All our stars are turning back to stone
This is waking to our morning
Falling through our floor
Our broken hearts as hard as broken bones

Sorrow says believe me
You can walk into my mouth
But every time we have it's hard to leave
Let's say it like the sunrise
When it's talking to the fog

We're both looking for a light
In the window of a house
Beneath our winter branches
Underneath our winter clouds
But it's hard to find

Lovers all surrender
Like the garden and the weeds
It's all we say when saying what we mean
Our arms are full of water
And the water all wants out
Like our meadow birds
giving back their wings

Sorrow says believe me
You can climb into my trees
We know it's harder to get down
each time we do
Let's say it like the sunrise
Talking to the fog

We're both listening for music
By a river after dark
In every space we're making
As we pull ourselves apart
But it's hard to find

Sorrow says believe me
You can beat into my breast
All our bandages and bruises know it's true
Let's say it to the sunrise
Its shaking us awake

We're both reaching out for love
Outside wanting in
To a room that's made of moonlight
And the walls are warm as skin
Where our memories of singing
Fill the air behind our heads
And our meadow bugs are living
For the only flowers left
Where our burns return their fire
And the cold can have our clothes
Where our dying deer is folded
On the soft side of the road
Where the wind is our direction
And the waves say come along
Where the faces of our family
And friends go on and on
But it's hard to find

Tears That Don't Matter

Open a door, hold hands
Empty your pockets
and get to know Jesus
Have a heart,
watch where you're going
That's where you'll see
enough blood for a lifetime

Play nice, learn a lesson
Fall apart
as easily as moonlight
Know what you want,
give it to someone
Spending their memory's
nickels and pennies

You're only as empty
as a lost and found
A cup with a crack,
a necklace to tangle
Only as true to life as a lost and found
Socks and a watch left in a lunchbox
Tears that don't matter now

Make time, die trying
Trust your gut if it's there for the taking
Look alive, don't listen
Anything worth it is said in cold water

Fly right, eat a rainbow
Speak of the devil
when God's in the details
Meet the moment, kill kindness
Finding and keeping
that pot you can piss in

So are you or are you not
the lost and found
A coat with a phone,
a crayon for breaking
Only as true to life
as a lost and found
A rock and roll key chain,
that wish you could whistle
And tears that don't matter now

What goes in
is never what comes out
That hole in a yard ball,
some pieces of seashell
You're only empty
as a lost and found

Sounds from a house,
the end of a candle
That kiss for your trouble,
ice and its goosebumps
All the runaway meanings
of keeping your hat on
The names and their bruises,
some eyes that got empty
One chance in a million,
the light where you lost her

The miles and a mother
shed like a snakeskin
Some shame and some anger
and all those drugs just for nothing

A swimming of colors
on a Japanese beetle
When the cynic within you
finally bowed to a daughter
And the sea and its reasoning
and the bones of your music
And that voice that you love
and the life you were dreaming
The doors that keep closing,
all the hands you let go of
And the tears that don't matter

Teeth in the Grass

And when you give me your clothes
And when we're lovers at last
Fresh air, perfume in your nose
There will be teeth in the grass

And when you give me your house
When we're all brothers at last
There will be food in our mouths
There will be teeth in the grass

And when there's nothing to want
When we're all brilliant and fast
When all tomorrows are gone
There will be teeth in the grass

This Solemn Day

Touch me while we both have hands
We won't keep them very long
Watch the window curtain blowing in the breeze
Keep your blessed memories

It's not what we talk about
When the table gossip turns
Someday you might find a circle of my friends
And they'll cry when you walk in

The grass is high on grandpa's farm
But he's not there to cut it down
Gray cat walking through the yard
Stops short and turns around as if he heard a sound

And we'll forgot this solemn day
We'll be always young again
But I'll remember him, the one who's left us now
And hold you close as you'll allow

Thomas County Law

Thomas County law's
got a crooked tooth
Every traffic light is red
when it tells the truth
The church bell isn't kidding
when it cries for you
Nobody looks away
when the sun goes down

Thomas County road
takes you where it will
Someone's singing on
the far side of other hills
There's nowhere safe to
bury all the time I've killed
Nobody looks away
when the sun goes down

There's a couple ways to cross
Thomas County line
You can't see beyond the trees,
they're too tall and wide
I never seem to see
around my brother's wife
Nobody looks away
when the sun goes down

There are castles for kings
There are birds without wings
I could whine about it all but I won't

Thomas County law's
got a crooked tooth
There ain't a mother with a heart
less than black and blue
When they hold them to the light
you can see right through
Every dreamer falls asleep
in their dancing shoes
I may say I don't belong here
but I know I do
Nobody looks away
when the sun goes down

"The Trapeze Swinger"

The director Paul Weitz called and wanted to use some songs from *Our Endless Numbered Days* in a movie he was making called *In Good Company*. But he said, "It'd be great if you had another song." I liked the challenge of writing for someone else, so he sent me the script and I took its themes as a place to start free-associating from.

I'd been sitting on the melody for a while, a repetitive, looping thing that felt almost religious to me, trancelike. Sometimes that works when you're telling a story, because in a way it never really ends until you decide to stop talking. There's always another loose thread to pick up and run with. I thought it would be fun to see how long I could sustain it. Plus, at the time I didn't know too many other chords. The lyrics came about when I was in Australia on tour, staying in a hotel tower that was several stories high. I was looking down on the streets of this foreign city, observing from the window and free-associating from the themes of the script. It really has nothing to do with the movie, just its own little cryptic story.

It's such a long song. It's incredible that it's become so beloved. There's a tendency with short songs to do more polishing because they have to say what they need to say in their small window of opportunity. They can end up taking much longer to write. Forever sometimes. Years. But this one took an afternoon. With the longer, freewheeling things, you feel fine just throwing paint at them. They're less precious. Maybe because you know there's going to be a lot more paint where that came from.

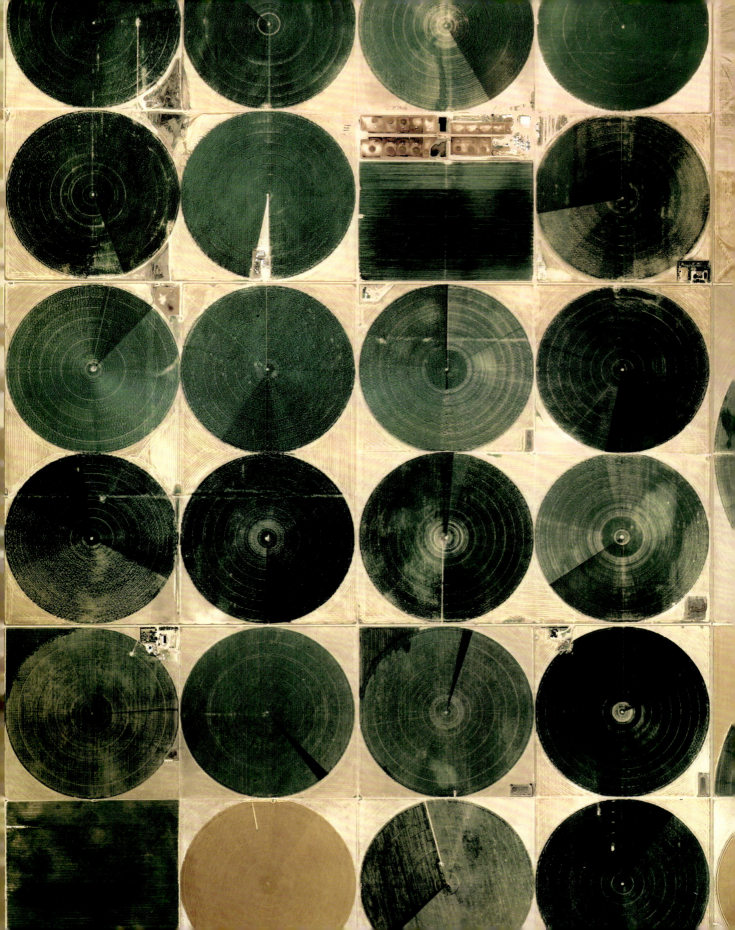

The Trapeze Swinger

Please remember me happily
By the rosebush laughing
With bruises on my chin, the time when
We counted every black car passing
Your house beneath the hill
And up until someone caught us in the kitchen
With maps, a mountain range, a piggy bank
A vision too removed to mention

But please remember me fondly
I heard from someone you're still pretty
And then they went on to say
That the pearly gates had some eloquent graffiti
Like "we'll meet again" and "fuck the man"
And "tell my mother not to worry"
And angels with their great handshakes
But always done in such a hurry

And please remember me that Halloween
Making fools of all the neighbors
Our faces painted white
By midnight, we'd forgotten one another
And when the morning came, I was ashamed
Only now it seems so silly
That season left the world and then returned
But now you're lit up by the city

So please remember me mistakenly
In the window of the tallest tower
Calling passersby but much too high
To see the empty road at happy hour
Gleam and resonate, just like the gates
Around the holy kingdom
With words like "lost and found" and "don't look down"
And "someone save temptation"

And please remember me as in the dream
We had as rug-burned babies
Among the fallen trees but fast asleep
Beside the lions and the ladies
That called you what you like and even might
Give a gift for your behavior
A fleeting chance to see a trapeze
Swinger high as any savior

But please remember me, my misery
And how it lost me all I wanted
Those dogs that love the rain and chasing trains
The colored birds above their running
In circles around the well and where it spells
On the wall behind St. Peter
So bright, on cinder gray, in spray paint
"Who the hell can see forever?"

And please remember me seldomly
In the car behind the carnival
My hand between your knees, you turned from me
And said, "The trapeze act was wonderful
But never meant to last," the clowns that passed
Saw me just come up with anger
When it filled with circus dogs, the parking lot
Had an element of danger

So please remember me finally
And all my uphill clawing
My dear, but if I make the pearly gates
I'll do my best to make a drawing
Of God and Lucifer, a boy and girl
An angel kissing on a sinner
A monkey and a man, a marching band
All around a frightened trapeze swinger

Tree by the River

Maryanne, do you remember
The tree by the river
When we were seventeen?
The dark canyon wall, the call and the answer
And the mare in the pasture
Pitch black and baring its teeth

I recall the sun in our faces
Stuck and leaning on graces
And being strangers to change
The radio and the bones we found frozen
All the thorns and the roses
Beneath your windowpane

Now I'm asleep in a car
I mean the world
To a potty-mouthed girl
And a pretty pair of blue-eyed birds
"Time isn't kind or unkind,"
You liked to say
But I wonder to who
And what it is you're saying today

Maryanne, do you remember
The tree by the river
When we were seventeen?
The dark canyon road, I was coy in the half moon
Happy just to be with you
And you were happy for me

The Truest Stars We Know

Someone gets to be the river
Someone is the sea
Someone gets to be the fire
Someone is the leaves
And someone's walking
into morning light
And calling to it cold
Everybody moves beneath
The truest stars they know

Jesus and his trophy wives
Are praying for the suicides and the orphans
Save us all from what we want
Beautiful and beaten back to life

Someone has a door to heaven
Someone has the lock
Someone has to be the dove
When someone is the hawk
And someone's talking to the mouths around
And hearing them for good
Everybody's branches falling
Harder than they should

And I know Jesus and his trophy wives
Are praying for the broken to be noticed
Save us all from what we want
Beautiful and beaten back to life

Two Hungry Blackbirds

Lovers accustomed to tragedy
See every kiss in the window across the street
Breezes and blessings passing by

I'm in the shade of the dogwood tree
Not the one where you told your name to me
Two hungry blackbirds laying nearby

If I could be over you when the sky starts falling
Would you be happy under me?
If I could be under you if the earth was burning
Could you be trusted over me?

Spoke to a mother whose baby drowned
Gave me advice or a rumor she once heard
"Heaven's a distance, not a place"

Gave her an ear from the corn we grew
You were away, but she gave her thanks to you
That was a year ago come May

If I could be over you when the sky starts falling
Would you be smothered under me?
If I could be under you if the earth was burning
Would you be crying over me?

I can hear kids in the yard next door
Cats in the brush when the calendar fell down
Wait by the shade tree one more year

Poetry tempered with tragedy
Tempted and pulled when you cry upon my sleeve
Two flocks of blackbirds meet the air

If I could be over you when the sky starts falling
Would you be happy under me?
If I could be under you if the earth was burning
could you be trusted over me?

Upward Over the Mountain

Mother, don't worry,
I killed the last snake that lived in the creek bed
Mother, don't worry,
I've got some money I saved for the weekend
Mother, remember
being so stern with that girl who was with me
Mother, remember
the blink of an eye when I breathed through your body

So may the sunrise bring hope
where it once was forgotten
Sons are like birds flying
upward over the mountain

Mother, I made it up
from the bruise on the floor of this prison
Mother, I lost it,
all of the fear of the Lord I was given
Mother, forget me
now that the creek drank the cradle you sang to
Mother, forgive me,
I sold your car for the shoes that I gave you

So may the sunrise bring hope
where it once was forgotten
Sons can be birds taken broken
up to the mountain

Mother, don't worry,
I've got a coat and some friends on the corner
Mother, don't worry,
she's got a garden we're planting together
Mother, remember
the night that the dog had her pups in the pantry
Blood on the floor,
fleas on their paws
And you cried 'til the morning

So may the sunrise bring hope
where it once was forgotten
Sons are like birds flying
always over the mountain

MOTHER DON'T WORRY

I KILLED THE LAST SNAKE THAT LIVED
IN THE CREEK BED
MOTHER DON'T WORRY
~~I'VE MADE A SONG OF MOST EVERYTHING~~
~~YOU'VE SAID~~
I'VE GOT SOME MONEY I SAVE FOR
THE WEEKEND

~~SO MAY THIS ONE GIVE YOU HOPE~~

MOTHER I REMEMBER
I WAS THE FIRST ONE TO BREATHE
THROUGH YOUR BODY

~~MO~~THER DON'T WORRY
~~I'~~VE GOT A COAT AND SOME
~~FR~~IENDS ON THE CORNER
~~MO~~THER DON'T WORRY
~~SH~~E'S GOT A GARDEN ~~THAT~~
~~CAN PLANT WITH HER~~
~~WE'~~RE PLANTING TOGETHER

SO MAY THE SUNRISE BRING ~~THE~~ HOPE
WHERE IT ONCE WAS FORGOTTEN

MOTHER REMEMBER
THE NIGHT ~~HE SHOT~~ ~~THAT THE DOG~~
~~KILLED THE DOG THE~~ ~~SHOTS~~
HAD HER PUPS IN THE PANTRY

~~BLOOD ON THE FLOOR, THE TEARS~~
~~ON OUR CHEEKS FOR THE~~
~~TWO NOT TO MAKE IT~~
BLOOD ON THE FLOOR A FLEA
ON MY LEG
AND YOU CRIED
TILL THE MORNING

SONS ARE LIKE BIRDS FLYING
UPWARDS OVER THE MOUNTAIN
ALWAYS   TAKEN BROKEN UP TO THE MOUNTAIN

Valentine

A house can get cold when there's no one to share
The sun in the kitchen, the creak on the stairs
The pictures of friends, crooked blurs on the walls
The pot of hydrangea alone in the hall

You were a breeze idly passing me by
That dropped in my lap like a stone from the sky
When I come home, now you're waiting right there
To offer an apple, a plum, or a pear

So close your eyes, Valentine
Cry to sleep some other time
Your burdens lie upon the ground
Between our shadows now

A house can get cold when there's no one to share
A weight on your conscience, a knot in your hair
Walk with me now and we'll seek our reward
In the simple contentments that time can afford

Close your eyes, Valentine
Cry to sleep some other time
Your burdens lie upon the ground
Between our shadows now

Wade Across the Water

Saw you wave across the river
Winter coat across your shoulders
Calling out, what did you say?
If I wade across the water
When I rise, will you be there
Open-armed or turned the other way?

Saw you wave across the river
Handkerchief in your fingers
Just in case, well, just in case
If I lose to the water
Lose it all for you, lover
You were all I wanted anyway

Walking Far from Home

I was walking far from home
Where the names were not burned along the wall
Saw a building high as heaven
But the door was so small

I saw rain clouds, little babies
And a bridge that had tumbled to the ground
I saw sinners making music
And I've dreamt of that sound

I was walking far from home
But I carried your letters all the while
I saw lovers in a window
Whisper, "Want me like time"

I saw sickness, blooming fruit trees
I saw blood and a bit of it was mine
I saw children in a river
But their lips were still dry

I was walking far from home
And I found your face mingled in the crowd
Saw a boatful of believers
Sail off, talking too loud

I saw sunlight on the water
Saw a bird fall like a hammer from the sky
An old woman on a speed train
She was closing her eyes

I saw flowers on a hillside
And a millionaire pissing on the lawn
Saw a prisoner take a pistol
And say, "Join me in song"

Saw a car crash in the country
Where the prayers run like weeds along the road
I saw strangers stealing kisses
Giving only their clothes

Saw a white dog chase its tail
And a pair of hearts carved into a stone
I saw kindness and an angel
Crying, "Take me back home"

Saw a highway, saw an ocean
I saw widows in the temple to the law
Naked dancers in the city
And they spoke for us all

I saw loaded linen tables
And a motherless colt, then it was gone
I saw hungry brothers waiting
With a radio on

I was walking far from home
Where the names were not burned along the wall
Saw a wet road form a circle
And it came like a call from the Lord

Waves of Galveston

Leave the waves of Galveston
but only if you can
'Cause you've been hid behind
the seawall gently folded in the sand
Papa left you for heaven
after your mama lost her song
And though your baby left you for Houston,
no one stays there very long

There's a graveyard by the pizza parlor,
a gate that only closes
Snowbirds fly away like secrets
no one really wants to know
The climbing moon's always shining
on the kind of shells you keep
The broken horse tied to the water tower's
running in his sleep

It's too bad that you ain't
got a soft place to fall
It's too bad Texas leans
to the least of us all and says,
"If you can make the music
Then you can have the dance
If you can shoot the pistol
Then you can wear the pants"

Leave the waves of Galveston
but only if you can
It's the only place the Lone Star
really offered you a hand
Your baby left you nothing
but a dog she left for dead
You never knew you were a burden
until it hit you on the head

It's too bad that you ain't
got a soft place to fall
It's too bad Texas leans
to the least in us all and says,
"If you can make the music
Then you can have the dance
If you can shoot the pistol
Then you can wear the pants"

Weary Memory

Found your mittens behind a box of pictures
You would wear them before I brewed the tea
That's one memory I can easily conjure
A weary memory I can always see

Found your rosary broken into pieces
Every night, by the bed, you'd kiss the beads
Those are moments that I can always relive
Weary memories I can always see

Found a photo of you when we were married
Leaning back on a broken willow tree
That's one memory that I choose to carry
A weary memory I can always see

Years to Burn
(with Calexico)

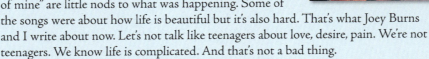

Calexico and I had been trying to clear the schedule and work together again ever since *In the Reins*, and this was finally the time. I had enjoyed working with Ben Bridwell and Jesca Hoop so much that I was eager to get into another collaborative experience. The first EP we'd done together was just songs I had lying around, plus we were just getting to know one another. This time, with all those years of experience, I was curious to write for my idea of what we could do. I composed for the ensemble.

It was just fun to cut loose and play with friends. Lines like "I followed the water and found these friends of mine" are little nods to what was happening. Some of the songs were about how life is beautiful but it's also hard. That's what Joey Burns and I write about now. Let's not talk like teenagers about love, desire, pain. We're not teenagers. We know life is complicated. And that's not a bad thing.

The phrase itself is ambiguous. Years to burn. If you say you've got years to burn, does that mean you have all the time in the world? Or does it mean you've been brutalized by life and you're condemned to years of feeling the pain? I like those open-ended phrases. They're like a portrait where you're not quite sure what the subject's expression is saying. It makes you want to keep coming back, trying to figure it out. When a phrase expresses itself too completely, there's no reason to keep engaging with it.

The last tune, "In Your Own Time," is one of my oldest songs—one of the first songs that people like Jonathan Poneman at Sub Pop heard—so doing it here was a nod to the format of *In the Reins*, breathing new life into those early demos. It was the end of the session at Matt Ross-Spang's studio in Nashville, and we needed one more song. My manager Howard Greynolds suggested this one, and I asked Joey to sing it. I think switching up the vocals makes it feel like more of a group and gives variety to the sequence of songs.

For the cover, I wanted to draw the three of us—Joey, John, and me. I tried a bunch of versions and concepts, but it wasn't really working. Then my wife, Kim, said, "Why not just throw them all in there?" It became a game to see what a pile of our faces looked like, like the painter Philip Guston's piles of legs or knees and feet. It's fun to have everybody in there, each our own cartoon character with our little signature looks.

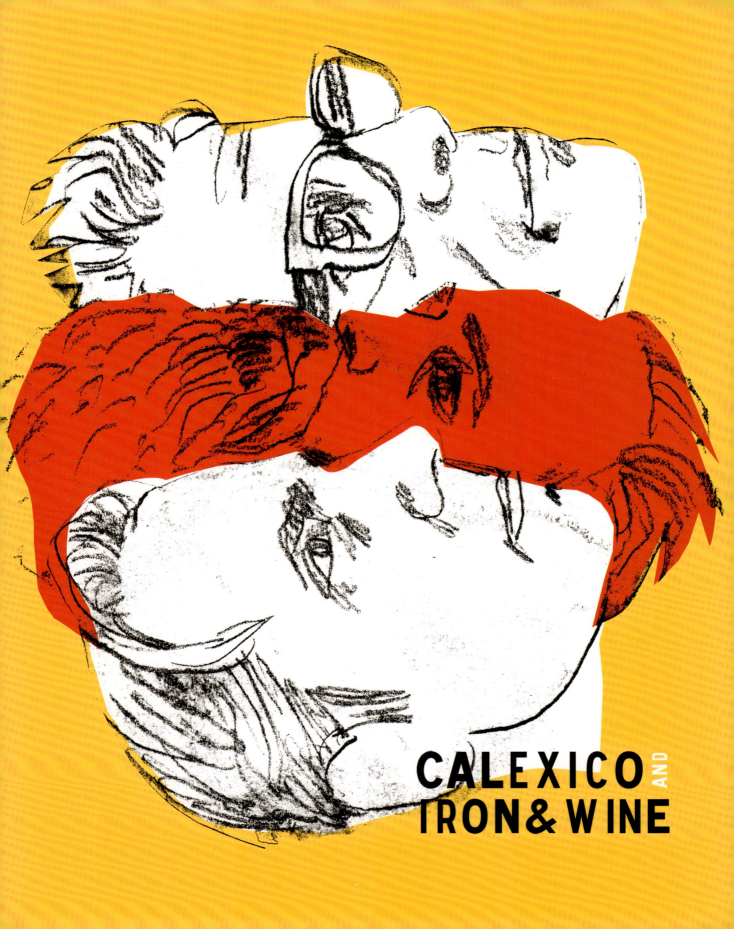

What Heaven's Left

You take these tears off my face
You give me dawn
for all the night that I make
What wave of a wild hand
called you into this world?

You take my fear and give me a fist
When I come to fight you come with a kiss
What wave of a wild hand
called you into this world?

I could be lost in the hills, laid on the street
And like the morning, you'd find me in time
Ask me what heaven's left
and I'll say, "Nothing comes to mind"

What wave of a wild hand
called you into this world?

I could be lost in the hills,
dead on my feet
And like morning you'd find me in time

You take my doubt and let me believe
You find the lightning in the tops of my trees
What blink of a wild eye
called you into this world?

You take my tongue
when I try to say
"I'm always coming home
the same castaway"
What wave of a wild hand
called you into this world?

I could be lost in the hills,
down on my knees
And like the morning you'll find me in time
Ask me what heaven's left
and I'll say, "Nothing comes to mind"

What Hurts Worse

Let's forget whatever we lost
Rolling around in the weeds
Finding ourselves broken
Looking for light on the floor

Let's become the lovers we want
Banging our heads in the fog
Flowers will close and open
Life going by like we care

One day it's whatever we made
From pieces off the side of a road
Marked on our map of what hurts
And what hurts worse

Let's become the lovers we need
Who knew we'd be needing so much?
We keep finding ourselves broken
Tossed in the yard with the bones

Let's forget whatever we know
Knowing all too little too late
Laying down in our own horizon
Letting that water hit home

White Tooth Man

Said the plainclothes cop to the beauty queen
"I've seen nothing but a spoke in the wheel"
So she gave up her crown to a kid with a crutch
And they both felt cheated after closing the deal
When the white tooth man I ran with then
Got all cut up from pissing out in the weeds
And a fight upstate with a broken blade
And a wife whose finger never wanted a ring

Said the plainclothes cop to the Indian chief
"I've made nothing but an honest mistake"
And the postman cried while reading your mail
And we all got trampled in the Christmas parade
When the white tooth man who sold me the gun
A map of Canaan, and a government bond
Said, "I love this town but it ain't the same"
His ski mask ripped as he was putting it on

Said the plainclothes cop to the Holy Ghost
"I've heard nothing yet that wasn't the wind"
And we all got sick on a strip club meal
While the statehouse pardoned all the witches again
So the white tooth man with his kids in the car
And a wad of money that was already spent
Said, "I love my dog but she just ran away
And she'll keep running like the world never ends"

Why Hate the Winter

All the water's run out, and you sit there wet
There's a high-speed chase on the TV set
And I think to myself, "Why hate the winter?"

The fireplace glows on the snow outside
You've a towel around your head and words in your eyes
They're the words I would say if only I was braver

But it's much too cold to run like a dog all alone
So come to my side and snuggle with me in the blanket
Don't offer your love, 'cause I'm not the one who should take it

I've battened the doors and the windows too
The radio man says it's negative two
Then he puts on a song that just wouldn't fit in the summer

Your body, it sways, it's so fragile and bare
You say, "Won't you come here and play in my hair?"
But I stand like a tree taken by a shiver

And it's much too cold to run like a dog all alone
So come to my side and snuggle with me in the blanket
Don't offer your love, 'cause I'm not the one who should take it

The floorboards are quiet and cold to the feet
And I cry like a child 'cause you've gone to sleep
I'd give you my soul if it wasn't that of a sinner

You're no Virgin Mary, no angel so clean
And there's no telling all the damage you've seen
But your skin makes for me a warm screaming reminder

That it's much too cold to run like a dog all alone
So come to my side and snuggle with me in the blanket
Don't offer your love, 'cause I'm not a man who can take it

The Wind Is Low

You, strong as a virgin birth
Me, keeping your every word
Two dots where a single was
Three, counting the little one

We sail in the smallest boat
Sleep just when the wind is low

You see from the sparrow's height
Me, seeking you every night
Two sailing towards the sun
Three, counting the little one

We sail in the smallest boat
Sleep just when the wind is low

Winter Prayers

Well, it's cold and you're bored
From counting the smart cars on 94
When you dream, you're back home
But the lakeside don't trust you to walk alone
Hollow trees talk offhand
All the neckties are toasting with empty cans
And you know why she's gone
Like the clothes in the river drifting on

Slide down south
'Cause once in a while
Your confidence leaves you like
Smoke falls out her red mouth

Well, she left you the holes
The tracks in the backyard December snow
But those sad souvenirs
They end at the fence line and disappear
Why'd you follow her there?
Milwaukee's a deaf ear for winter prayers
There's no night, there's no day
With only hope in your pocket and hell to pay

Slide down south
When once in a while
Your confidence leaves you like
Smoke falls out her red mouth

Wolves
(Song of the Shepherd's Dog)

Wolves by the road
and a bike wheel spinning on a pawnshop wall
She'll wring out her colored hair
like a butterfly beaten in a summer rainfall
And then roll on the kitchen floor
of some fucker with a pocketful of foreign change
The song of the shepherd's dog,
a ditch in the dark
In the ear of the lamb who's going
to try to run away
Whoever got that brave

Wolves in the middle of town
and a chapel bell ringing through the windblown trees
She'll wave to the butcher's boy
with the parking lot music everybody believes
And then dive like a dying bird
at any dude with a dollar at the penny arcade
The song of the shepherd's dog,
the waiter and the check
Or the rooster on a rooftop
waiting for day
And you know what he's going to say

Wolves at the end of the bed
and a postcard hidden in her winter clothes
She'll weep in the back of a truck
to the traitors only trying to find her bullet hole
And then run down a canopy road
to some mother and a baby with a cross to bear
The song of the shepherd's dog,
a little brown flea
In the bottle of oil for your wool,
wild hair
You'll never get him out of there

Woman King

Blackbird claw, raven wing
Under the red sunlight
Long clothesline, two shirtsleeves
Waving as we go by

Hundred years, hundred more
Someday we may see a
Woman king, wristwatch time
Slowing as she goes to sleep

Black horsefly, lemonade
Jar on the red ant hill
Garden worm, cigarette
Ash on the windowsill

Hundred years, hundred more
Someday we may see a
Woman king, sword in hand
Swing at some evil and bleed

Black hoof mare, broken leg
Eye on the shotgun shell
Age old dog, hornet nest
Built in the big church bell

Hundred years, hundred more
Someday we may see a
Woman king, bloodshot eye
Thumb down and starting to weep

Years to Burn

A night to believe
To touch on your tongue
A lover to slow you down
To see by the moon
Like robins in rain
And want what the world's holding out

Years to burn, years to burn
Breezes that die and rise
Years to burn, years to burn
Our tears hold the light in our eyes

A night to be born
And another to find
The music across the street
A friend in its arms
Their breath in the cold
Disappears like a snake in the weeds

Years to burn, years to burn
Breezes that die and rise
Years to burn, years to burn
Our tears hold the light in our eyes

Light Verse

I went through a period where the writing was down to a trickle. With the COVID pandemic and all that uncertainty and chaos, I felt pretty low, even when I sat down to write. I don't write out of a place of tension or chaos or anxiety, so it was creatively devastating for me. I'm not going to say that I wasn't scared that it would dry up, because it's a muscle that you have to keep working. But I couldn't fight it, so I just got busy doing other things. I played guitar and made a lot of artwork. I let go of songwriting for a little while and hoped that later it would come back. And it did, slowly, just as the world started to open up and heal in its own chaotic way. Sometimes you have to go live life and have something else to write about.

Part of it was going to Memphis and recording an EP of Lori McKenna covers. I felt eager to get back into recording something, but I didn't have enough of my own songs. She's a great writer, and I'd been listening to her on repeat. That's what was on my mind. It reminded me how much I enjoy the process. Home recording was really the gateway to my career—and it was my first love—so being back in the studio reminded me of that. And it got me thinking about the little bits and pieces of songs that I had, in a way that I wasn't before.

Then I started playing shows and reconnecting with the audience. I went on tour with Andrew Bird. I haven't had a whole lot of musical community in my career—because I've lived in the middle of nowhere, had a bunch of kids, and have never really been part of a scene—so it was really fun to hang with him. Our careers are shaped a bit similarly, and he's just so talented. It was great to have a kindred spirit. All of those elements together got me back on track, and on the other side of that tour, it was on. I went home, and it was pretty much all writing, all the time for a while.

The idea of making the album in LA took root in my mind. Sebastian had been in my ear for years about recording with Dave Way, and I'm so glad that I did. Being there in January and February was great, and the whole LA talent bank is no joke.

I had met Tyler Chester because he plays keys in Bird's band, and I knew I wanted to work with him. Tyler's a secret weapon who adds weight to a tune, but in a way that's almost transparent, subliminal, very powerful. Paul Cartwright is a super talented string player and arranger. I wanted to mine all the Brazilian records I love for the way they use strings, whether larger orchestras or small chamber groups, to express the range of emotions in a story without being syrupy. But also, because he grew up in Bakersfield, Paul can rock some country mandolin. So he was all over the place. And Davíd Garza can play anything. He played lots of slide guitar, which balances the elegance of some of the string sections and brings it back down to a folksy, bluesy thing. And lots of percussion. With the Stones, Brian Jones always picked the right sound to help the tune find its identity. Davíd is that kind of player.

With all these guys, their sounds started to feel like characters in a play. They didn't really play the changes; they played the emotional tones of what was happening in the song, as if the song happened invisibly and they played around it. And they had a grasp on any references I'd throw out. I could say Nick Drake's "River Man," and they'd know exactly where to go. I'd say Big Star and they'd go, "Oh yeah, I got you." Joni Mitchell, they'd know exactly what that palette is, the tone and approach that I was talking about. It was a really freeing space to be in, because we loved all those elemental artists. We loved those individual palettes so much, but we were interested in seeing what happened when you threw them all together.

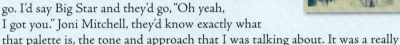

I didn't have a real specific idea of what the songs would be about, but I knew I wanted to be a bit lighter in touch. I wouldn't say they're silly songs, but they have silly elements, silly wordplay, and silly rhymes. I always enjoyed that about Harry Nilsson or Randy Newman records. Or even the Beatles. They're really funny. I like songs that exist in both worlds—they can be poignant, but not all doom and gloom. For some reason, when I sit down to write a song, I usually feel like I have to say what I mean instead of joking around like I normally do in everyday conversation. This time it felt better to just let the songs go where they went and not really pull them back to the somber place.

"Bag of Cats" and "Sweet Talk" are both punchy and irreverent, but they're also just dumb and playful. "Sucker punching straight into the face of a wonderful life" . . . what does that even mean? I remember that "wonderful life" phrase popping up and then just letting my imagination run free. Imagining a wonderful life as a person and trying to engage with it in whatever way you can. Sometimes acquiescing, sometimes trying to snuggle up with it, sometimes sneaking around behind its back or taking it for granted. I was just having fun, really. I felt like the more disrespectful I was to the concept of a wonderful life, the more interesting it was!

The lyric for "Anyone's Game" is another playful one. I sat on the melody for more than a decade in different iterations until I found a series of poems by the Serbian poet Vasko Popa—translated by Charles Simic—who's a hero of mine. You never know when a song is going to click with you and suddenly start making demands. I try to hold on to melodies the best I can, but timing is everything. In the short poems, Popa wrote rules for imaginary children's games in a way that felt like they were both a nonsensical dream and a portrait of human existence at the same time. The poem about a game called Wedding starts with "each strips his own skin / each bares his own constellation / which has never seen the night."

But if this record is about anything, it's about loss. "Taken by Surprise" is a pretty direct one. To me, it sounds like a Mickey Newbury song, very quiet and still and very sentimental. It lays out a story and the pain of it all in a very simple way, yet alluding to a lot of unsaid things. If you've experienced the sort of loss of innocence it describes, you recognize it immediately. I think a song can be sad, but you enjoy it because it sounds familiar.

The Hoop record taught me that if you turn anything into a duet, it gets more interesting. "All in Good Time" piles up contradictions—we succeeded and we failed, we kissed and we knifed each other in the back. But the meaning changes completely when you start trading lines. It insinuates subtext and drama. It starts to feel like life. Fiona Apple is a huge inspiration to me, so I felt really blessed that she sang on it. What she contributed changed the song totally, expanding it to make it so much more complex than anything I had written. Because it's a little bit low for her register, I think you can feel both the vulnerability and the strength of her voice even more.

As far as lyrical approach and emotional tone, the centerpiece of the record for me is "You Never Know." It's the sort of song that creates itself as it goes. It repeats that opening line "You could make . . ." and it can go anywhere. That's a creative energy that I like, an expressive and positive way of moving through life. Creating the future as you go. What's next? You never know.

Yellow Jacket

Doves are losing lucky feathers in the sky
Appaloosas in the moonlight going blind
What a cold world for such a long life
Dogs are barking on the record every night

A dream can close its tired eyes
An old tear can roll itself away
If that's all we lose tonight
And the cold goes back in its bones
Let those bells ring themselves true

Your aurora borealis turning green
Stopped your bitchin' motorcycle with a tree
What's a cold world to butterfly wings
Get to know your yellow jacket by the sting

Dreams close their tired eyes
Old tears roll themselves away
If that's all we lose tonight
And the cold goes back in its bones
Let those bells ring themselves true

You Never Know

You could make gray and call it gold
Let it fool your eyes
You could make rain and let it have your life
Being green grass, any little wind
Begs you for a dance
You could say love until it lasts

You could make good, there's a lot of ways
With nowhere left to go
Let it be the song on your little radio
You could make light, be the silly word
Sitting on a tongue
You could make nice or beat a drum

Don't you wanna know how far you're gonna go
Fickle as tomorrow talking to a wind chime
Folding your hands, empty as glass
Waiting to break
Don't you wanna know how close you're gonna get
Kissing like people stepping on flowers
Wishing on stars empty as glass
Waiting to break

You could have a heart until it's pouring out
If it's in your blood
You could make waves and then you better run
Being black cloud, there's a lot to say
And so much room to grow
You could make rain, you never know

You could make gray and call it gold
Let it fool your eyes
Follow any wave crashing down to size
You could be wrong, don't you wanna know
Deep into the night
Like a little stone thrown across ice

Your Fake Name Is Good Enough for Me

Your fake watch is in your broken hand
Barely keeping time
Barefoot in the city and your phone is ringing
Met you watching all the happy kids
Climbing on a car
They were singing something
maybe they were singing,
"Become the weeds, we will become
Become the sea, we will become"

Your fake money gave you everything
Left along the road
You're cursing by the furnace
and your phone is ringing
Met you watching all the happy kids
Clapping in the cold
They were singing something
maybe they were singing,
"Become the weeds, we will become
Become the sea, we will become"

Your fake name is not for everyone
But good enough for me
Forgotten by the garden
and your phone is ringing
Met you watching all the happy kids
Kiss each other clean
They were singing something
maybe they were singing,
"Become the weeds, we will become
Become the sea, we will become"

"We will become the rising sun
We will become the damage done
We will become the river's sway
We will become the love we made
We will become the endless chain
We will become the forgotten name
We will become the sinner and saint
We will become the bandage and the blade
We will become the word and the breath
We will become the card and the chest
We will become the liked and the loathed
We will become the bruise and the blow
We will become the fruit and the fall
We will become the caress and the claw
We will become the glory and the guilt
We will become the blossom and the wilt
We will become both right and wrong
We will become the sound and the song
We will become the tooth and the tongue
We will become the target and the gun
We will become so cruel and kind
We will become the wary and the wild
We will become allegiance and doubt
We will become the whisper and the shout
We will become the honest and the veiled
We will become the hammer and the nail
We will become the blessing and the curse
We will become but it could be worse
We will become the blood and the bone
We will become an ice cream cone
We will become the way and the wall
We will become a disco ball
We will become both now and then
We will become again and again"

Your Sly Smile

Blue light sitting lotus-style
On your A-frame in the countryside
Stillness slides the door and walks inside

Candle on the windowsill
Burned wickless through our low-lit meal
Heaven only knows the things you hide

In your blue eyes
And your sly smile

Tangerine on both your hands
Smells strong as the tobacco can
Roll me up a smoke if you don't mind
Touch me like that afternoon
When your friends would all be over soon
And you said, "What the hell, we'll make the time"

With your blue eyes
And your sly smile

Index by Album

The Creek Drank the Cradle
2002

The Creek Drank the Cradle
   Commentary   *6*

Lion's Mane	*138*
Bird Stealing Bread	*29*
Faded from the Winter	*82*
Promising Light	*184*
The Rooster Moans	*197*
Upward Over the Mountain	*246*
Southern Anthem	*214*
An Angry Blade	*13*
Weary Memory	*253*
Promise What You Will	*183*
Muddy Hymnal	*165*

The Sea & the Rhythm
2003

Beneath the Balcony	*25*
The Sea and the Rhythm	*199*
The Night Descending	*173*
Jesus the Mexican Boy	*119*
Someday the Waves	*212*

Our Endless Numbered Days
2005

Our Endless Numbered Days
   Commentary   *54*

On Your Wings	*175*
Naked as We Came	*168*
Cinder and Smoke	*56*
Sunset Soon Forgotten	*224*
Teeth in the Grass	*235*
Love and Some Verses	*142*
Radio War	*191*
Each Coming Night	*72*
Free Until They Cut Me Down	*90*
Fever Dream	*85*
Sodom, South Georgia	*210*
Passing Afternoon	*178*

Woman King
2005

Woman King Commentary   *76*

Woman King	*266*
Jezebel	*120*
Gray Stables	*102*
Freedom Hangs Like Heaven	*91*
My Lady's House	*166*
Evening on the Ground (Lilith's Song)	*79*

In the Reins (with Calexico)
2005

In the Reins Commentary	106
He Lays in the Reins	108
Prison on Route 41	182
A History of Lovers	112
Red Dust	192
Sixteen, Maybe Less	208
Burn That Broken Bed	41
Dead Man's Will	64

The Shepherd's Dog
2007

The Shepherd's Dog Commentary	128
Pagan Angel and a Borrowed Car	177
White Tooth Man	260
Lovesong of the Buzzard	145
Carousel	49
House by the Sea	116
Innocent Bones	118
Wolves (Song of the Shepherd's Dog)	264
Resurrection Fern	193
Boy with a Coin	38
The Devil Never Sleeps	68
Peace Beneath the City	179
Flightless Bird, American Mouth	86

Around the Well
2009

"The Trapeze Swinger" Commentary	238

DISC 1

Dearest Forsaken	65
Morning	164
Loud as Hope	141
Peng! 33 (Stereolab)	
Sacred Vision	198
Friends They Are Jewels	93
Hickory	111
Waitin' for a Superman (The Flaming Lips)	
Swans and the Swimming	225
Call Your Boys	46
Such Great Heights (The Postal Service)	

DISC 2

Communion Cups and Someone's Coat	60
Belated Promise Ring	23
God Made the Automobile	96
Homeward, These Shoes	113
Love Vigilantes (New Order)	
Sinning Hands	207
No Moon	174
Serpent Charmer	200
Carried Home	50
Kingdom of the Animals	132
Arms of a Thief	16
The Trapeze Swinger	240

Kiss Each Other Clean
2011

Kiss Each Other Clean Commentary	160
Walking Far from Home	250
Me and Lazarus	150
Tree by the River	243
Monkeys Uptown	163
Half Moon	104
Rabbit Will Run	188
Godless Brother in Love	97
Big Burned Hand	28
Glad Man Singing	94
Your Fake Name Is Good Enough for Me	274

B-SIDES

Summer in Savannah	222
Biting Your Tail	30
Black Candle	37
Lean into the Light	136

Ghost on Ghost
2013

Ghost on Ghost Commentary	204
Caught in the Briars	53
The Desert Babbler	66
Joy	125
Low Light Buddy of Mine	149
Grace for Saints and Ramblers	98
Grass Widows	101
Singers and the Endless Song	206
Sundown (Back in the Briars)	223
Winter Prayers	263
New Mexico's No Breeze	170
Lovers' Revolution	146
Baby Center Stage	20

B-SIDES

Next to Paradise	171
My Side of the Road	167
Dirty Dream	71

Archive Series Volume No. 1
2015

Slow Black River	209
The Wind Is Low	262
Eden	74
Two Hungry Blackbirds	245
Freckled Girl	89
Judgement	127
Sing Song Bird	203
Beyond the Fence	26
Quarters in a Pocket	187
Loretta	140
Everyone's Summer of '95	80
Minor Piano Keys	154
Your Sly Smile	276
Halfway to Richmond	105
Wade Across the Water	249
Postcard	180

Beast Epic
2017

Beast Epic / Weed Garden Commentary	218
Claim Your Ghost	58
Thomas County Law	237
Bitter Truth	34
Song in Stone	213
Summer Clouds	220
Call It Dreaming	42
About a Bruise	9
Last Night	133
Right for Sky	194
The Truest Stars We Know	244
Our Light Miles	176

DELUXE PRESSING

Hearts Walk Anywhere	109
Kicking the Old Rain	130

Archive Series Volume No. 3
2017

Stranger Lay Beside Me	216
Miss Bottom of the Hill	156

Weed Garden
2018

Beast Epic / Weed Garden Commentary	218
What Hurts Worse	259
Waves of Galveston	252
Last of Your Rock 'n' Roll Heroes	135
Milkweed	153
Autumn Town Leaves	19
Talking to Fog	230

Years to Burn (with Calexico)
2019

Years to Burn Commentary	256
What Heaven's Left	258
Midnight Sun	
Father Mountain	84
Outside El Paso (Instrumental)	
Follow the Water	88
The Bitter Suite	33
Years to Burn	267
In Your Own Time	117

Archive Series Volume No. 5: Tallahassee Recordings
2021

Why Hate the Winter	261
This Solemn Day	236
Loaning Me Secrets	139
John's Glass Eye	124
Calm on the Valley	48
Ex-Lover Lucy Jones	81
Elizabeth	75
Show Him the Ground	202
Straight and Tall	215
Cold Town	59
Valentine	248

Light Verse
2024

Light Verse Commentary	268
You Never Know	273
Anyone's Game	15
All in Good Time	10
Cutting It Close	63
Taken by Surprise	228
Yellow Jacket	272
Sweet Talk	227
Tears That Don't Matter	232
Bag of Cats	22
Angels Go Home	14

About the Author

Sam Beam is a singer-songwriter who has been creating music as Iron & Wine for over two decades. Through the course of ten albums, numerous EPs and singles, and the initial volumes of an archive series, Iron & Wine has captured the emotion and imagination of listeners with distinctly cinematic songs.

Song Credits

About A Bruise
Words and Music by Sam Beam
© 2017 SAM BEAM MUSIC
All Rights Administered by WARNER-
TAMERLANE PUBLISHING CORP.
All Rights Reserved Used by Permission
Reprinted by Permission of Hal Leonard LLC

All In Good Time
Words and Music by Sam Beam
© 2024 SAM BEAM MUSIC
All Rights Administered by WARNER-
TAMERLANE PUBLISHING CORP.
All Rights Reserved Used by Permission
Reprinted by Permission of Hal Leonard LLC

Angels Go Home
Words and Music by Sam Beam
© 2024 SAM BEAM MUSIC
All Rights Administered by WARNER-
TAMERLANE PUBLISHING CORP.
All Rights Reserved Used by Permission
Reprinted by Permission of Hal Leonard LLC

An Angry Blade
Words and Music by Sam Beam
© 2002 SAM BEAM MUSIC
All Rights Administered by WARNER-
TAMERLANE PUBLISHING CORP.
All Rights Reserved Used by Permission
Reprinted by Permission of Hal Leonard LLC

Anyone's Game
Words and Music by Sam Beam
© 2024 SAM BEAM MUSIC
All Rights Administered by WARNER-
TAMERLANE PUBLISHING CORP.
All Rights Reserved Used by Permission
Reprinted by Permission of Hal Leonard LLC

Arms Of A Thief
Words and Music by Sam Beam
© 2007 SAM BEAM MUSIC
All Rights Administered by WARNER-
TAMERLANE PUBLISHING CORP.
All Rights Reserved Used by Permission
Reprinted by Permission of Hal Leonard LLC

Autumn Town Leaves
Words and Music by Sam Beam
© 2018 SAM BEAM MUSIC
All Rights Administered by WARNER-
TAMERLANE PUBLISHING CORP.
All Rights Reserved Used by Permission
Reprinted by Permission of Hal Leonard LLC

Baby Center Stage
Words and Music by Sam Beam
© 2013 SAM BEAM MUSIC
All Rights Administered by WARNER-
TAMERLANE PUBLISHING CORP.
All Rights Reserved Used by Permission
Reprinted by Permission of Hal Leonard LLC

Bag Of Cats
Words and Music by Sam Beam
© 2024 SAM BEAM MUSIC
All Rights Administered by WARNER-
TAMERLANE PUBLISHING CORP.
All Rights Reserved Used by Permission
Reprinted by Permission of Hal Leonard LLC

Belated Promise Ring
Words and Music by Sam Beam
© 2004 SAM BEAM MUSIC
All Rights Administered by WARNER-
TAMERLANE PUBLISHING CORP.
All Rights Reserved Used by Permission
Reprinted by Permission of Hal Leonard LLC

Beneath The Balcony
Words and Music by Sam Beam
© 2003 SAM BEAM MUSIC
All Rights Administered by WARNER-
TAMERLANE PUBLISHING CORP.
All Rights Reserved Used by Permission
Reprinted by Permission of Hal Leonard LLC

Beyond The Fence
Words and Music by Sam Beam
© 2015 SAM BEAM MUSIC
All Rights Administered by WARNER-
TAMERLANE PUBLISHING CORP.
All Rights Reserved Used by Permission
Reprinted by Permission of Hal Leonard LLC

Big Burned Hand
Words and Music by Sam Beam
© 2011 SAM BEAM MUSIC
All Rights Administered by WARNER-
TAMERLANE PUBLISHING CORP.
All Rights Reserved Used by Permission
Reprinted by Permission of Hal Leonard LLC

Bird Stealing Bread
Words and Music by Sam Beam
© 2002 SAM BEAM MUSIC
All Rights Administered by WARNER-
TAMERLANE PUBLISHING CORP.
All Rights Reserved Used by Permission
Reprinted by Permission of Hal Leonard LLC

Biting Your Tail
Words and Music by Sam Beam
© 2010 SAM BEAM MUSIC
All Rights Administered by WARNER-
TAMERLANE PUBLISHING CORP.
All Rights Reserved Used by Permission
Reprinted by Permission of Hal Leonard LLC

Bitter Truth
Words and Music by Sam Beam
© 2017 SAM BEAM MUSIC
All Rights Administered by WARNER-
TAMERLANE PUBLISHING CORP.
All Rights Reserved Used by Permission
Reprinted by Permission of Hal Leonard LLC

Black Candle
Words and Music by Sam Beam
© 2011 SAM BEAM MUSIC
All Rights Administered by WARNER-
TAMERLANE PUBLISHING CORP.
All Rights Reserved Used by Permission
Reprinted by Permission of Hal Leonard LLC

Boy With A Coin
Words and Music by Sam Beam
© 2007 SAM BEAM MUSIC
All Rights Administered by WARNER-
TAMERLANE PUBLISHING CORP.
All Rights Reserved Used by Permission
Reprinted by Permission of Hal Leonard LLC

Burn That Broken Bed
Words and Music by Sam Beam
© 2005 SAM BEAM MUSIC
All Rights Administered by WARNER-
TAMERLANE PUBLISHING CORP.
All Rights Reserved Used by Permission
Reprinted by Permission of Hal Leonard LLC

Call It Dreaming
Words and Music by Sam Beam
© 2017 SAM BEAM MUSIC
All Rights Administered by WARNER-
TAMERLANE PUBLISHING CORP.
All Rights Reserved Used by Permission
Reprinted by Permission of Hal Leonard LLC

Call Your Boys
Words and Music by Sam Beam
© 2009 SAM BEAM MUSIC
All Rights Administered by WARNER-
TAMERLANE PUBLISHING CORP.
All Rights Reserved Used by Permission
Reprinted by Permission of Hal Leonard LLC

Calm On The Valley
Words and Music by Sam Beam
© 2021 SAM BEAM MUSIC
All Rights Administered by WARNER-
TAMERLANE PUBLISHING CORP.
All Rights Reserved Used by Permission
Reprinted by Permission of Hal Leonard LLC

Carousel
Words and Music by Sam Beam
© 2007 SAM BEAM MUSIC
All Rights Administered by WARNER-
TAMERLANE PUBLISHING CORP.
All Rights Reserved Used by Permission
Reprinted by Permission of Hal Leonard LLC

Carried Home
Words and Music by Sam Beam
© 2009 SAM BEAM MUSIC
All Rights Administered by WARNER-
TAMERLANE PUBLISHING CORP.
All Rights Reserved Used by Permission
Reprinted by Permission of Hal Leonard LLC

Communion Cups And Someone's Coat
Words and Music by Sam Beam
© 2009 SAM BEAM MUSIC
All Rights Administered by WARNER-
TAMERLANE PUBLISHING CORP.
All Rights Reserved Used by Permission
Reprinted by Permission of Hal Leonard LLC

Caught In The Briars
Words and Music by Sam Beam
© 2013 SAM BEAM MUSIC
All Rights Administered by WARNER-
TAMERLANE PUBLISHING CORP.
All Rights Reserved Used by Permission
Reprinted by Permission of Hal Leonard LLC

Cinder And Smoke
Words and Music by Sam Beam
© 2004 SAM BEAM MUSIC
All Rights Administered by WARNER-
TAMERLANE PUBLISHING CORP.
All Rights Reserved Used by Permission
Reprinted by Permission of Hal Leonard LLC

Claim Your Ghost
Words and Music by Sam Beam
© 2017 SAM BEAM MUSIC
All Rights Administered by WARNER-
TAMERLANE PUBLISHING CORP.
All Rights Reserved Used by Permission
Reprinted by Permission of Hal Leonard LLC

Cold Town
Words and Music by Sam Beam
© 2021 SAM BEAM MUSIC
All Rights Administered by WARNER-
TAMERLANE PUBLISHING CORP.
All Rights Reserved Used by Permission
Reprinted by Permission of Hal Leonard LLC

Cutting It Close
Words and Music by Sam Beam
© 2024 SAM BEAM MUSIC
All Rights Administered by WARNER-
TAMERLANE PUBLISHING CORP.
All Rights Reserved Used by Permission
Reprinted by Permission of Hal Leonard LLC

Dead Man's Will
Words and Music by Sam Beam
© 2005 SAM BEAM MUSIC
All Rights Administered by WARNER-
TAMERLANE PUBLISHING CORP.
All Rights Reserved Used by Permission
Reprinted by Permission of Hal Leonard LLC

Dearest Forsaken
Words and Music by Sam Beam
© 2009 SAM BEAM MUSIC
All Rights Administered by WARNER-
TAMERLANE PUBLISHING CORP.
All Rights Reserved Used by Permission
Reprinted by Permission of Hal Leonard LLC

The Desert Babbler
Words and Music by Sam Beam
© 2013 SAM BEAM MUSIC
All Rights Administered by WARNER-
TAMERLANE PUBLISHING CORP.
All Rights Reserved Used by Permission
Reprinted by Permission of Hal Leonard LLC

Dirty Dream
Words and Music by Sam Beam
© 2013 SAM BEAM MUSIC
All Rights Administered by WARNER-
TAMERLANE PUBLISHING CORP.
All Rights Reserved Used by Permission
Reprinted by Permission of Hal Leonard LLC

Each Coming Night
Words and Music by Sam Beam
© 2004 SAM BEAM MUSIC
All Rights Administered by WARNER-
TAMERLANE PUBLISHING CORP.
All Rights Reserved Used by Permission
Reprinted by Permission of Hal Leonard LLC

Eden
Words and Music by Sam Beam
© 2015 SAM BEAM MUSIC
All Rights Administered by WARNER-
TAMERLANE PUBLISHING CORP.
All Rights Reserved Used by Permission
Reprinted by Permission of Hal Leonard LLC

Elizabeth
Words and Music by Sam Beam
© 2021 SAM BEAM MUSIC
All Rights Administered by WARNER-
TAMERLANE PUBLISHING CORP.
All Rights Reserved Used by Permission
Reprinted by Permission of Hal Leonard LLC

Evening On The Ground (Lilith's Song)
Words and Music by Sam Beam
© 2005 SAM BEAM MUSIC
All Rights Administered by WARNER-
TAMERLANE PUBLISHING CORP.
All Rights Reserved Used by Permission
Reprinted by Permission of Hal Leonard LLC

Everyone's Summer Of '95
Words and Music by Sam Beam
© 2015 SAM BEAM MUSIC
All Rights Administered by WARNER-
TAMERLANE PUBLISHING CORP.
All Rights Reserved Used by Permission
Reprinted by Permission of Hal Leonard LLC

Ex-Lover Lucy Jones
Words and Music by Sam Beam
© 2021 SAM BEAM MUSIC
All Rights Administered by WARNER-
TAMERLANE PUBLISHING CORP.
All Rights Reserved Used by Permission
Reprinted by Permission of Hal Leonard LLC

Faded From The Winter
Words and Music by Sam Beam
© 2002 SAM BEAM MUSIC
All Rights Administered by WARNER-
TAMERLANE PUBLISHING CORP.
All Rights Reserved Used by Permission
Reprinted by Permission of Hal Leonard LLC

Father Mountain
Words and Music by Sam Beam
© 2019 SAM BEAM MUSIC
All Rights Administered by WARNER-
TAMERLANE PUBLISHING CORP.
All Rights Reserved Used by Permission
Reprinted by Permission of Hal Leonard LLC

Fever Dream
Words and Music by Sam Beam
© 2004 SAM BEAM MUSIC
All Rights Administered by WARNER-
TAMERLANE PUBLISHING CORP.
All Rights Reserved Used by Permission
Reprinted by Permission of Hal Leonard LLC

Flightless Bird, American Mouth
Words and Music by Sam Beam
© 2007 SAM BEAM MUSIC
All Rights Administered by WARNER-
TAMERLANE PUBLISHING CORP.
All Rights Reserved Used by Permission
Reprinted by Permission of Hal Leonard LLC

Follow The Water
Words and Music by Sam Beam
© 2019 SAM BEAM MUSIC
All Rights Administered by WARNER-
TAMERLANE PUBLISHING CORP.
All Rights Reserved Used by Permission
Reprinted by Permission of Hal Leonard LLC

Freckled Girl
Words and Music by Sam Beam
© 2015 SAM BEAM MUSIC
All Rights Administered by WARNER-
TAMERLANE PUBLISHING CORP.
All Rights Reserved Used by Permission
Reprinted by Permission of Hal Leonard LLC

Free Until They Cut Me Down
Words and Music by Sam Beam
© 2004 SAM BEAM MUSIC
All Rights Administered by WARNER-
TAMERLANE PUBLISHING CORP.
All Rights Reserved Used by Permission
Reprinted by Permission of Hal Leonard LLC

Freedom Hangs Like Heaven
Words and Music by Sam Beam
© 2005 SAM BEAM MUSIC
All Rights Administered by WARNER-
TAMERLANE PUBLISHING CORP.
All Rights Reserved Used by Permission
Reprinted by Permission of Hal Leonard LLC

Friends They Are Jewels
Words and Music by Sam Beam
© 2009 SAM BEAM MUSIC
All Rights Administered by WARNER-
TAMERLANE PUBLISHING CORP.
All Rights Reserved Used by Permission
Reprinted by Permission of Hal Leonard LLC

Glad Man Singing
Words and Music by Sam Beam
© 2011 SAM BEAM MUSIC
All Rights Administered by WARNER-
TAMERLANE PUBLISHING CORP.
All Rights Reserved Used by Permission
Reprinted by Permission of Hal Leonard LLC

God Made The Automobile
Words and Music by Sam Beam
© 2009 SAM BEAM MUSIC
All Rights Administered by WARNER-
TAMERLANE PUBLISHING CORP.
All Rights Reserved Used by Permission
Reprinted by Permission of Hal Leonard LLC

Godless Brother In Love
Words and Music by Sam Beam
© 2011 SAM BEAM MUSIC
All Rights Administered by WARNER-
TAMERLANE PUBLISHING CORP.
All Rights Reserved Used by Permission
Reprinted by Permission of Hal Leonard LLC

Grace For Saints And Ramblers
Words and Music by Sam Beam
© 2013 SAM BEAM MUSIC
All Rights Administered by WARNER-
TAMERLANE PUBLISHING CORP.
All Rights Reserved Used by Permission
Reprinted by Permission of Hal Leonard LLC

Grass Windows
Words and Music by Sam Beam
© 2013 SAM BEAM MUSIC
All Rights Administered by WARNER-
TAMERLANE PUBLISHING CORP.
All Rights Reserved Used by Permission
Reprinted by Permission of Hal Leonard LLC

Gray Stables
Words and Music by Sam Beam
© 2005 SAM BEAM MUSIC
All Rights Administered by WARNER-
TAMERLANE PUBLISHING CORP.
All Rights Reserved Used by Permission
Reprinted by Permission of Hal Leonard LLC

Half Moon
Words and Music by Sam Beam
© 2011 SAM BEAM MUSIC
All Rights Administered by WARNER-
TAMERLANE PUBLISHING CORP.
All Rights Reserved Used by Permission
Reprinted by Permission of Hal Leonard LLC

Halfway To Richmond
Words and Music by Sam Beam
© 2015 SAM BEAM MUSIC
All Rights Administered by WARNER-
TAMERLANE PUBLISHING CORP.
All Rights Reserved Used by Permission
Reprinted by Permission of Hal Leonard LLC

He Lays In The Reins
Words and Music by Sam Beam
© 2005 SAM BEAM MUSIC
All Rights Administered by WARNER-
TAMERLANE PUBLISHING CORP.
All Rights Reserved Used by Permission
Reprinted by Permission of Hal Leonard LLC

Hearts Walk Anywhere
Words and Music by Sam Beam
© 2017 SAM BEAM MUSIC
All Rights Administered by WARNER-
TAMERLANE PUBLISHING CORP.
All Rights Reserved Used by Permission
Reprinted by Permission of Hal Leonard LLC

Hickory
Words and Music by Sam Beam
© 2009 SAM BEAM MUSIC
All Rights Administered by WARNER-
TAMERLANE PUBLISHING CORP.
All Rights Reserved Used by Permission
Reprinted by Permission of Hal Leonard LLC

A History Of Lovers
Words and Music by Sam Beam
© 2005 SAM BEAM MUSIC
All Rights Administered by WARNER-
TAMERLANE PUBLISHING CORP.
All Rights Reserved Used by Permission
Reprinted by Permission of Hal Leonard LLC

Homeward
Words and Music by Sam Beam
© 2009 SAM BEAM MUSIC
All Rights Administered by WARNER-
TAMERLANE PUBLISHING CORP.
All Rights Reserved Used by Permission
Reprinted by Permission of Hal Leonard LLC

House By The Sea
Words and Music by Sam Beam
© 2007 SAM BEAM MUSIC
All Rights Administered by WARNER-
TAMERLANE PUBLISHING CORP.
All Rights Reserved Used by Permission
Reprinted by Permission of Hal Leonard LLC

In Your Own Time
Words and Music by Sam Beam
© 2019 SAM BEAM MUSIC
All Rights Administered by WARNER-
TAMERLANE PUBLISHING CORP.
All Rights Reserved Used by Permission
Reprinted by Permission of Hal Leonard LLC

Innocent Bones
Words and Music by Sam Beam
© 2007 SAM BEAM MUSIC
All Rights Administered by WARNER-
TAMERLANE PUBLISHING CORP.
All Rights Reserved Used by Permission
Reprinted by Permission of Hal Leonard LLC

Jesus The Mexican Boy
Words and Music by Sam Beam
© 2003 SAM BEAM MUSIC
All Rights Administered by WARNER-
TAMERLANE PUBLISHING CORP.
All Rights Reserved Used by Permission
Reprinted by Permission of Hal Leonard LLC

Jezebel
Words and Music by Sam Beam
© 2005 SAM BEAM MUSIC
All Rights Administered by WARNER-
TAMERLANE PUBLISHING CORP.
All Rights Reserved Used by Permission
Reprinted by Permission of Hal Leonard LLC

John's Glass Eye
Words and Music by Sam Beam
© 2021 SAM BEAM MUSIC
All Rights Administered by WARNER-
TAMERLANE PUBLISHING CORP.
All Rights Reserved Used by Permission
Reprinted by Permission of Hal Leonard LLC

Joy
Words and Music by Sam Beam
© 2013 SAM BEAM MUSIC
All Rights Administered by WARNER-
TAMERLANE PUBLISHING CORP.
All Rights Reserved Used by Permission
Reprinted by Permission of Hal Leonard LLC

Judgement
Words and Music by Sam Beam
© 2015 SAM BEAM MUSIC
All Rights Administered by WARNER-
TAMERLANE PUBLISHING CORP.
All Rights Reserved Used by Permission
Reprinted by Permission of Hal Leonard LLC

Kicking The Old Rain
Words and Music by Sam Beam
© 2017 SAM BEAM MUSIC
All Rights Administered by WARNER-
TAMERLANE PUBLISHING CORP.
All Rights Reserved Used by Permission
Reprinted by Permission of Hal Leonard LLC

Kingdom Of The Animals
Words and Music by Sam Beam
© 2009 SAM BEAM MUSIC
All Rights Administered by WARNER-
TAMERLANE PUBLISHING CORP.
All Rights Reserved Used by Permission
Reprinted by Permission of Hal Leonard LLC

Last Night
Words and Music by Sam Beam
© 2017 SAM BEAM MUSIC
All Rights Administered by WARNER-
TAMERLANE PUBLISHING CORP.
All Rights Reserved Used by Permission
Reprinted by Permission of Hal Leonard LLC

Last Of Your Rock 'N' Roll Heroes
Words and Music by Sam Beam
© 2018 SAM BEAM MUSIC
All Rights Administered by WARNER-
TAMERLANE PUBLISHING CORP.
All Rights Reserved Used by Permission
Reprinted by Permission of Hal Leonard LLC

Lean Into The Light
Words and Music by Sam Beam
© 2011 SAM BEAM MUSIC
All Rights Administered by WARNER-
TAMERLANE PUBLISHING CORP.
All Rights Reserved Used by Permission
Reprinted by Permission of Hal Leonard LLC

Lion's Mane
Words and Music by Sam Beam
© 2002 SAM BEAM MUSIC
All Rights Administered by WARNER-
TAMERLANE PUBLISHING CORP.
All Rights Reserved Used by Permission
Reprinted by Permission of Hal Leonard LLC

Loaning Me Secrets
Words and Music by Sam Beam
© 2021 SAM BEAM MUSIC
All Rights Administered by WARNER-
TAMERLANE PUBLISHING CORP.
All Rights Reserved Used by Permission
Reprinted by Permission of Hal Leonard LLC

Loretta
Words and Music by Sam Beam
© 2015 SAM BEAM MUSIC
All Rights Administered by WARNER-
TAMERLANE PUBLISHING CORP.
All Rights Reserved Used by Permission
Reprinted by Permission of Hal Leonard LLC

Loud As Hope
Words and Music by Sam Beam
© 2009 SAM BEAM MUSIC
All Rights Administered by WARNER-
TAMERLANE PUBLISHING CORP.
All Rights Reserved Used by Permission
Reprinted by Permission of Hal Leonard LLC

Love And Some Verses
Words and Music by Sam Beam
© 2004 SAM BEAM MUSIC
All Rights Administered by WARNER-
TAMERLANE PUBLISHING CORP.
All Rights Reserved Used by Permission
Reprinted by Permission of Hal Leonard LLC

Lovers' Revolution
Words and Music by Sam Beam
© 2013 SAM BEAM MUSIC
All Rights Administered by WARNER-
TAMERLANE PUBLISHING CORP.
All Rights Reserved Used by Permission
Reprinted by Permission of Hal Leonard LLC

Lovesong Of The Buzzard
Words and Music by Sam Beam
© 2007 SAM BEAM MUSIC
All Rights Administered by WARNER-
TAMERLANE PUBLISHING CORP.
All Rights Reserved Used by Permission
Reprinted by Permission of Hal Leonard LLC

Low Light Buddy Of Mine
Words and Music by Sam Beam
© 2013 SAM BEAM MUSIC
All Rights Administered by WARNER-
TAMERLANE PUBLISHING CORP.
All Rights Reserved Used by Permission
Reprinted by Permission of Hal Leonard LLC

Me And Lazarus
Words and Music by Sam Beam
© 2011 SAM BEAM MUSIC
All Rights Administered by WARNER-
TAMERLANE PUBLISHING CORP.
All Rights Reserved Used by Permission
Reprinted by Permission of Hal Leonard LLC

Milkweed
Words and Music by Sam Beam
© 2018 SAM BEAM MUSIC
All Rights Administered by WARNER-
TAMERLANE PUBLISHING CORP.
All Rights Reserved Used by Permission
Reprinted by Permission of Hal Leonard LLC

Minor Piano Keys
Words and Music by Sam Beam
© 2015 SAM BEAM MUSIC
All Rights Administered by WARNER-
TAMERLANE PUBLISHING CORP.
All Rights Reserved Used by Permission
Reprinted by Permission of Hal Leonard LLC

Miss Bottom Of The Hill
Words and Music by Sam Beam
© 2017 SAM BEAM MUSIC
All Rights Administered by WARNER-
TAMERLANE PUBLISHING CORP.
All Rights Reserved Used by Permission
Reprinted by Permission of Hal Leonard LLC

Monkeys Uptown
Words and Music by Sam Beam
© 2011 SAM BEAM MUSIC
All Rights Administered by WARNER-
TAMERLANE PUBLISHING CORP.
All Rights Reserved Used by Permission
Reprinted by Permission of Hal Leonard LLC

Morning
Words and Music by Sam Beam
© 2009 SAM BEAM MUSIC
All Rights Administered by WARNER-
TAMERLANE PUBLISHING CORP.
All Rights Reserved Used by Permission
Reprinted by Permission of Hal Leonard LLC

Muddy Hymnal
Words and Music by Sam Beam
© 2002 SAM BEAM MUSIC
All Rights Administered by WARNER-
TAMERLANE PUBLISHING CORP.
All Rights Reserved Used by Permission
Reprinted by Permission of Hal Leonard LLC

My Lady's House
Words and Music by Sam Beam
© 2005 SAM BEAM MUSIC
All Rights Administered by WARNER-
TAMERLANE PUBLISHING CORP.
All Rights Reserved Used by Permission
Reprinted by Permission of Hal Leonard LLC

My Side Of The Road
Words and Music by Sam Beam
© 2015 SAM BEAM MUSIC
All Rights Administered by WARNER-
TAMERLANE PUBLISHING CORP.
All Rights Reserved Used by Permission
Reprinted by Permission of Hal Leonard LLC

Naked As We Came
Words and Music by Sam Beam
© 2004 SAM BEAM MUSIC
All Rights Administered by WARNER-
TAMERLANE PUBLISHING CORP.
All Rights Reserved Used by Permission
Reprinted by Permission of Hal Leonard LLC

New Mexico's No Breeze
Words and Music by Sam Beam
© 2013 SAM BEAM MUSIC
All Rights Administered by WARNER-
TAMERLANE PUBLISHING CORP.
All Rights Reserved Used by Permission
Reprinted by Permission of Hal Leonard LLC

Next To Paradise
Words and Music by Sam Beam
© 2013 SAM BEAM MUSIC
All Rights Administered by WARNER-
TAMERLANE PUBLISHING CORP.
All Rights Reserved Used by Permission
Reprinted by Permission of Hal Leonard LLC

The Night Descending
Words and Music by Sam Beam
© 2003 SAM BEAM MUSIC
All Rights Administered by WARNER-
TAMERLANE PUBLISHING CORP.
All Rights Reserved Used by Permission
Reprinted by Permission of Hal Leonard LLC

No Moon
Words and Music by Sam Beam
© 2009 SAM BEAM MUSIC
All Rights Administered by WARNER-
TAMERLANE PUBLISHING CORP.
All Rights Reserved Used by Permission
Reprinted by Permission of Hal Leonard LLC

On Your Wings
Words and Music by Sam Beam
© 2004 SAM BEAM MUSIC
All Rights Administered by WARNER-
TAMERLANE PUBLISHING CORP.
All Rights Reserved Used by Permission
Reprinted by Permission of Hal Leonard LLC

Our Light Miles
Words and Music by Sam Beam
© 2017 SAM BEAM MUSIC
All Rights Administered by WARNER-
TAMERLANE PUBLISHING CORP.
All Rights Reserved Used by Permission
Reprinted by Permission of Hal Leonard LLC

Pagan Angel And A Borrowed Car
Words and Music by Sam Beam
© 2007 SAM BEAM MUSIC
All Rights Administered by WARNER-
TAMERLANE PUBLISHING CORP.
All Rights Reserved Used by Permission
Reprinted by Permission of Hal Leonard LLC

Passing Afternoon
Words and Music by Sam Beam
© 2004 SAM BEAM MUSIC
All Rights Administered by WARNER-
TAMERLANE PUBLISHING CORP.
All Rights Reserved Used by Permission
Reprinted by Permission of Hal Leonard LLC

Peace Beneath The City
Words and Music by Sam Beam
© 2007 SAM BEAM MUSIC
All Rights Administered by WARNER-
TAMERLANE PUBLISHING CORP.
All Rights Reserved Used by Permission
Reprinted by Permission of Hal Leonard LLC

Postcard
Words and Music by Sam Beam
© 2015 SAM BEAM MUSIC
All Rights Administered by WARNER-
TAMERLANE PUBLISHING CORP.
All Rights Reserved Used by Permission
Reprinted by Permission of Hal Leonard LLC

Prison On Route 41
Words and Music by Sam Beam
© 2005 SAM BEAM MUSIC
All Rights Administered by WARNER-
TAMERLANE PUBLISHING CORP.
All Rights Reserved Used by Permission
Reprinted by Permission of Hal Leonard LLC

Promise What You Will
Words and Music by Sam Beam
© 2002 SAM BEAM MUSIC
All Rights Administered by WARNER-
TAMERLANE PUBLISHING CORP.
All Rights Reserved Used by Permission
Reprinted by Permission of Hal Leonard LLC

Promising Light
Words and Music by Sam Beam
© 2002 SAM BEAM MUSIC
All Rights Administered by WARNER-
TAMERLANE PUBLISHING CORP.
All Rights Reserved Used by Permission
Reprinted by Permission of Hal Leonard LLC

Quarters In A Pocket
Words and Music by Sam Beam
© 2015 SAM BEAM MUSIC
All Rights Administered by WARNER-
TAMERLANE PUBLISHING CORP.
All Rights Reserved Used by Permission
Reprinted by Permission of Hal Leonard LLC

Rabbit Will Run
Words and Music by Sam Beam
© 2011 SAM BEAM MUSIC
All Rights Administered by WARNER-
TAMERLANE PUBLISHING CORP.
All Rights Reserved Used by Permission
Reprinted by Permission of Hal Leonard LLC

Radio War
Words and Music by Sam Beam
© 2004 SAM BEAM MUSIC
All Rights Administered by WARNER-
TAMERLANE PUBLISHING CORP.
All Rights Reserved Used by Permission
Reprinted by Permission of Hal Leonard LLC

Red Dust
Words and Music by Sam Beam
© 2005 SAM BEAM MUSIC
All Rights Administered by WARNER-
TAMERLANE PUBLISHING CORP.
All Rights Reserved Used by Permission
Reprinted by Permission of Hal Leonard LLC

Resurrection Fern
Words and Music by Sam Beam
© 2007 SAM BEAM MUSIC
All Rights Administered by WARNER-
TAMERLANE PUBLISHING CORP.
All Rights Reserved Used by Permission
Reprinted by Permission of Hal Leonard LLC

Right For Sky
Words and Music by Sam Beam
© 2017 SAM BEAM MUSIC
All Rights Administered by WARNER-
TAMERLANE PUBLISHING CORP.
All Rights Reserved Used by Permission
Reprinted by Permission of Hal Leonard LLC

The Rooster Moans
Words and Music by Sam Beam
© 2002 SAM BEAM MUSIC
All Rights Administered by WARNER-
TAMERLANE PUBLISHING CORP.
All Rights Reserved Used by Permission
Reprinted by Permission of Hal Leonard LLC

Sacred Vision
Words and Music by Sam Beam
© 2009 SAM BEAM MUSIC
All Rights Administered by WARNER-
TAMERLANE PUBLISHING CORP.
All Rights Reserved Used by Permission
Reprinted by Permission of Hal Leonard LLC

The Sea And The Rhythm
Words and Music by Sam Beam
© 2003 SAM BEAM MUSIC
All Rights Administered by WARNER-
TAMERLANE PUBLISHING CORP.
All Rights Reserved Used by Permission
Reprinted by Permission of Hal Leonard LLC

Serpent Charmer
Words and Music by Sam Beam
© 2009 SAM BEAM MUSIC
All Rights Administered by WARNER-
TAMERLANE PUBLISHING CORP.
All Rights Reserved Used by Permission
Reprinted by Permission of Hal Leonard LLC

Show Him The Ground
Words and Music by Sam Beam
© 2021 SAM BEAM MUSIC
All Rights Administered by WARNER-
TAMERLANE PUBLISHING CORP.
All Rights Reserved Used by Permission
Reprinted by Permission of Hal Leonard LLC

Sing Song Bird
Words and Music by Sam Beam
© 2015 SAM BEAM MUSIC
All Rights Administered by WARNER-
TAMERLANE PUBLISHING CORP.
All Rights Reserved Used by Permission
Reprinted by Permission of Hal Leonard LLC

Singers And The Endless Song
Words and Music by Sam Beam
© 2013 SAM BEAM MUSIC
All Rights Administered by WARNER-
TAMERLANE PUBLISHING CORP.
All Rights Reserved Used by Permission
Reprinted by Permission of Hal Leonard LLC

Sinning Hands
Words and Music by Sam Beam
© 2009 SAM BEAM MUSIC
All Rights Administered by WARNER-
TAMERLANE PUBLISHING CORP.
All Rights Reserved Used by Permission
Reprinted by Permission of Hal Leonard LLC

Sixteen
Words and Music by Sam Beam
© 2005 SAM BEAM MUSIC
All Rights Administered by WARNER-
TAMERLANE PUBLISHING CORP.
All Rights Reserved Used by Permission
Reprinted by Permission of Hal Leonard LLC

Slow Black River
Words and Music by Sam Beam
© 2015 SAM BEAM MUSIC
All Rights Administered by WARNER-
TAMERLANE PUBLISHING CORP.
All Rights Reserved Used by Permission
Reprinted by Permission of Hal Leonard LLC

Sodom, South Georgia
Words and Music by Sam Beam
© 2004 SAM BEAM MUSIC
All Rights Administered by WARNER-
TAMERLANE PUBLISHING CORP.
All Rights Reserved Used by Permission
Reprinted by Permission of Hal Leonard LLC

Someday The Waves
Words and Music by Sam Beam
© 2003 SAM BEAM MUSIC
All Rights Administered by WARNER-
TAMERLANE PUBLISHING CORP.
All Rights Reserved Used by Permission
Reprinted by Permission of Hal Leonard LLC

Song In Stone
Words and Music by Sam Beam
© 2017 SAM BEAM MUSIC
All Rights Administered by WARNER-
TAMERLANE PUBLISHING CORP.
All Rights Reserved Used by Permission
Reprinted by Permission of Hal Leonard LLC

Southern Anthem
Words and Music by Sam Beam
© 2002 SAM BEAM MUSIC
All Rights Administered by WARNER-
TAMERLANE PUBLISHING CORP.
All Rights Reserved Used by Permission
Reprinted by Permission of Hal Leonard LLC

Straight And Tall
Words and Music by Sam Beam
© 2021 SAM BEAM MUSIC
All Rights Administered by WARNER-
TAMERLANE PUBLISHING CORP.
All Rights Reserved Used by Permission
Reprinted by Permission of Hal Leonard LLC

A Stranger Lay Beside Me
Words and Music by Sam Beam
© 2017 SAM BEAM MUSIC
All Rights Administered by WARNER-
TAMERLANE PUBLISHING CORP.
All Rights Reserved Used by Permission
Reprinted by Permission of Hal Leonard LLC

Summer Clouds
Words and Music by Sam Beam
© 2017 SAM BEAM MUSIC
All Rights Administered by WARNER-
TAMERLANE PUBLISHING CORP.
All Rights Reserved Used by Permission
Reprinted by Permission of Hal Leonard LLC

Summer In Savannah
Words and Music by Sam Beam
© 2010 SAM BEAM MUSIC
All Rights Administered by WARNER-
TAMERLANE PUBLISHING CORP.
All Rights Reserved Used by Permission
Reprinted by Permission of Hal Leonard LLC

Sundown (Back In The Briars)
Words and Music by Sam Beam
© 2013 SAM BEAM MUSIC
All Rights Administered by WARNER-
TAMERLANE PUBLISHING CORP.
All Rights Reserved Used by Permission
Reprinted by Permission of Hal Leonard LLC

Sunset Soon Forgotten
Words and Music by Sam Beam
© 2004 SAM BEAM MUSIC
All Rights Administered by WARNER-
TAMERLANE PUBLISHING CORP.
All Rights Reserved Used by Permission
Reprinted by Permission of Hal Leonard LLC

Swans And The Swimming
Words and Music by Sam Beam
© 2009 SAM BEAM MUSIC
All Rights Administered by WARNER-
TAMERLANE PUBLISHING CORP.
All Rights Reserved Used by Permission
Reprinted by Permission of Hal Leonard LLC

Sweet Talk
Words and Music by Sam Beam
© 2024 SAM BEAM MUSIC
All Rights Administered by WARNER-
TAMERLANE PUBLISHING CORP.
All Rights Reserved Used by Permission
Reprinted by Permission of Hal Leonard LLC

Taken By Surprise
Words and Music by Sam Beam
© 2024 SAM BEAM MUSIC
All Rights Administered by WARNER-
TAMERLANE PUBLISHING CORP.
All Rights Reserved Used by Permission
Reprinted by Permission of Hal Leonard LLC

Talking To Fog
Words and Music by Sam Beam
© 2018 SAM BEAM MUSIC
All Rights Administered by WARNER-
TAMERLANE PUBLISHING CORP.
All Rights Reserved Used by Permission
Reprinted by Permission of Hal Leonard LLC

Tears That Don't Matter
Words and Music by Sam Beam
© 2024 SAM BEAM MUSIC
All Rights Administered by WARNER-
TAMERLANE PUBLISHING CORP.
All Rights Reserved Used by Permission
Reprinted by Permission of Hal Leonard LLC

Teeth In The Grass
Words and Music by Sam Beam
© 2004 SAM BEAM MUSIC
All Rights Administered by WARNER-
TAMERLANE PUBLISHING CORP.
All Rights Reserved Used by Permission
Reprinted by Permission of Hal Leonard LLC

The Bitter Suite: Evil Eye
Words and Music by Joseph G. Burns
and Sam Beam
Copyright © 2019 Lunada Bay and
Sam Beam Music
All Rights for Lunada Bay Administered by BMG
Rights Management (US) LLC
All Rights for Sam Beam Music Administered by
Warner-Tamerlane Publishing Corp.
All Rights Reserved Used by Permission

The Bitter Suite: Tennessee Train
Words and Music by Sam Beam
© 2019 SAM BEAM MUSIC
All Rights Administered by WARNER-
TAMERLANE PUBLISHING CORP.
All Rights Reserved Used by Permission
Reprinted by Permission of Hal Leonard LLC

The Bitter Suite: Pájaro
Words and Music by Joseph G. Burns
and Sam Beam
Copyright © 2019 Lunada Bay and
Sam Beam Music
All Rights for Lunada Bay Administered by BMG
Rights Management (US) LLC
All Rights for Sam Beam Music Administered by
Warner-Tamerlane Publishing Corp.
All Rights Reserved Used by Permission
Reprinted by Permission of Hal Leonard LLC

The Devil Never Sleeps
Words and Music by Sam Beam
© 2007 SAM BEAM MUSIC
All Rights Administered by WARNER-
TAMERLANE PUBLISHING CORP.
All Rights Reserved Used by Permission
Reprinted by Permission of Hal Leonard LLC

The Wind Is Low
Words and Music by Sam Beam
© 2015 SAM BEAM MUSIC
All Rights Administered by WARNER-
TAMERLANE PUBLISHING CORP.
All Rights Reserved Used by Permission
Reprinted by Permission of Hal Leonard LLC

This Solemn Day
Words and Music by Sam Beam
© 2021 SAM BEAM MUSIC
All Rights Administered by WARNER-
TAMERLANE PUBLISHING CORP.
All Rights Reserved Used by Permission
Reprinted by Permission of Hal Leonard LLC

Thomas County Law
Words and Music by Sam Beam
© 2017 SAM BEAM MUSIC
All Rights Administered by WARNER-
TAMERLANE PUBLISHING CORP.
All Rights Reserved Used by Permission
Reprinted by Permission of Hal Leonard LLC

The Trapeze Swinger
Words and Music by Sam Beam
© 2004 SAM BEAM MUSIC
All Rights Administered by WARNER-
TAMERLANE PUBLISHING CORP.
All Rights Reserved Used by Permission
Reprinted by Permission of Hal Leonard LLC

Tree By The River
Words and Music by Sam Beam
© 2011 SAM BEAM MUSIC
All Rights Administered by WARNER-
TAMERLANE PUBLISHING CORP.
All Rights Reserved Used by Permission
Reprinted by Permission of Hal Leonard LLC

The Truest Stars We Know
Words and Music by Sam Beam
© 2017 SAM BEAM MUSIC
All Rights Administered by WARNER-
TAMERLANE PUBLISHING CORP.
All Rights Reserved Used by Permission
Reprinted by Permission of Hal Leonard LLC

Two Hungry Blackbirds
Words and Music by Sam Beam
© 2015 SAM BEAM MUSIC
All Rights Administered by WARNER-
TAMERLANE PUBLISHING CORP.
All Rights Reserved Used by Permission
Reprinted by Permission of Hal Leonard LLC

Upward Over The Mountain
Words and Music by Sam Beam
© 2002 SAM BEAM MUSIC
All Rights Administered by WARNER-
TAMERLANE PUBLISHING CORP.
All Rights Reserved Used by Permission
Reprinted by Permission of Hal Leonard LLC

Valentine
Words and Music by Sam Beam
© 2021 SAM BEAM MUSIC
All Rights Administered by WARNER-
TAMERLANE PUBLISHING CORP.
All Rights Reserved Used by Permission
Reprinted by Permission of Hal Leonard LLC

Wade Across The Water
Words and Music by Sam Beam
© 2015 SAM BEAM MUSIC
All Rights Administered by WARNER-
TAMERLANE PUBLISHING CORP.
All Rights Reserved Used by Permission
Reprinted by Permission of Hal Leonard LLC

Walking Far From Home
Words and Music by Sam Beam
© 2011 SAM BEAM MUSIC
All Rights Administered by WARNER-
TAMERLANE PUBLISHING CORP.
All Rights Reserved Used by Permission
Reprinted by Permission of Hal Leonard LLC

Waves Of Galveston
Words and Music by Sam Beam
© 2018 SAM BEAM MUSIC
All Rights Administered by WARNER-
TAMERLANE PUBLISHING CORP.
All Rights Reserved Used by Permission
Reprinted by Permission of Hal Leonard LLC

Weary Memory
Words and Music by Sam Beam
© 2002 SAM BEAM MUSIC
All Rights Administered by WARNER-
TAMERLANE PUBLISHING CORP.
All Rights Reserved Used by Permission
Reprinted by Permission of Hal Leonard LLC

What Heaven's Left
Words and Music by Sam Beam
© 2019 SAM BEAM MUSIC
All Rights Administered by WARNER-
TAMERLANE PUBLISHING CORP.
All Rights Reserved Used by Permission
Reprinted by Permission of Hal Leonard LLC

What Hurts Worse
Words and Music by Sam Beam
© 2018 SAM BEAM MUSIC
All Rights Administered by WARNER-
TAMERLANE PUBLISHING CORP.
All Rights Reserved Used by Permission
Reprinted by Permission of Hal Leonard LLC

White Tooth Man
Words and Music by Sam Beam
© 2007 SAM BEAM MUSIC
All Rights Administered by WARNER-
TAMERLANE PUBLISHING CORP.
All Rights Reserved Used by Permission
Reprinted by Permission of Hal Leonard LLC

Why Hate The Winter
Words and Music by Sam Beam
© 2021 SAM BEAM MUSIC
All Rights Administered by WARNER-
TAMERLANE PUBLISHING CORP.
All Rights Reserved Used by Permission
Reprinted by Permission of Hal Leonard LLC

Winter Prayers
Words and Music by Sam Beam
© 2013 SAM BEAM MUSIC
All Rights Administered by WARNER-
TAMERLANE PUBLISHING CORP.
All Rights Reserved Used by Permission
Reprinted by Permission of Hal Leonard LLC

Wolves (Song Of The Shepherd's Dog)
Words and Music by Sam Beam
© 2007 SAM BEAM MUSIC
All Rights Administered by WARNER-
TAMERLANE PUBLISHING CORP.
All Rights Reserved Used by Permission
Reprinted by Permission of Hal Leonard LLC

Woman King
Words and Music by Sam Beam
© 2005 SAM BEAM MUSIC
All Rights Administered by WARNER-
TAMERLANE PUBLISHING CORP.
All Rights Reserved Used by Permission
Reprinted by Permission of Hal Leonard LLC

Years To Burn
Words and Music by Sam Beam
© 2019 SAM BEAM MUSIC
All Rights Administered by WARNER-
TAMERLANE PUBLISHING CORP.
All Rights Reserved Used by Permission
Reprinted by Permission of Hal Leonard LLC

Yellow Jacket
Words and Music by Sam Beam
© 2024 SAM BEAM MUSIC
All Rights Administered by WARNER-
TAMERLANE PUBLISHING CORP.
All Rights Reserved Used by Permission
Reprinted by Permission of Hal Leonard LLC

You Never Know
Words and Music by Sam Beam
© 2024 SAM BEAM MUSIC
All Rights Administered by WARNER-
TAMERLANE PUBLISHING CORP.
All Rights Reserved Used by Permission
Reprinted by Permission of Hal Leonard LLC

Your Fake Name Is Good Enough For Me
Words and Music by Sam Beam
© 2011 SAM BEAM MUSIC
All Rights Administered by WARNER-
TAMERLANE PUBLISHING CORP.
All Rights Reserved Used by Permission
Reprinted by Permission of Hal Leonard LLC

Your Sly Smile
Words and Music by Sam Beam
© 2015 SAM BEAM MUSIC
All Rights Administered by WARNER-
TAMERLANE PUBLISHING CORP.
All Rights Reserved Used by Permission
Reprinted by Permission of Hal Leonard LLC

weldon**owen**

an imprint of Insight Editions
PO Box 3088
San Rafael, CA 94912
www.weldonowen.com

CEO Raoul Goff
VP Publisher Roger Shaw
Publishing Director Katie Killebrew
Editor Peter Adrian Behravesh
Assistant Editor Amanda Nelson
VP, Creative Director Chrissy Kwasnik
Art Director and Designer Allister Fein
VP Manufacturing Alix Nicholaeff
Sr Production Manager Joshua Smith
Sr Production Manager, Subsidiary Rights Lina s Palma-Temena

Weldon Owen would also like to thank Howard Greynolds, Tarina Aumiller, Anders Smith Lindall, and Karen Levy.

Images on pages 2, 152, 172, 185, 196, 221, and 270 © Kim Black; Images on pages 8, 52, and 277 © Josh Wool; Images on pages 12, 24, 46, 70, 121, and 162 © Piper Ferguson; Images on pages 27, 78, 103, and 201 © Dusty Summers; Image on page 21 © Frida Clements; Image on page 32 © Jay Ryan/Bird Machine; Image on page 43 © Austin Wilson; Image on page 62 © Jesus Cisneros; Image on page 131 © Knoxy Knox (embroidery by Fort Lonesome); Images on pages 51 and 137 © Dan Grzeca; Image on page 186 © Nathaniel Russell; Image on page 239 © Karen Kurycki; Image on page 282 © Cherie Hansson; Image on page 40 © Dennis Kleiman; Image on page 155 © Joshua Mellin

Image on page 126: American Folk Art Museum / Gavin Ashworth / Art Resource, NY

Image on page 159: American Folk Art Museum / Scott Bowron / Art Resource, NY

Image on back cover: American Folk Art Museum / John Parnell / Art Resource, NY

All images not specified above © Sam Beam
Text © Sam Beam

Every effort was made to credit artists and photographers correctly. If you would like to update a credit, please contact the publisher.

All rights reserved. No part of this book may be reproduced in any form without written permission from the publisher.

ISBN: 979-8-88674-203-9

Manufactured in China by Insight Editions
10 9 8 7 6 5 4 3 2 1

Insight Editions, in association with Roots of Peace, will plant two trees for each tree used in the manufacturing of this book. Roots of Peace is an internationally renowned humanitarian organization dedicated to eradicating land mines worldwide and converting war-torn lands into productive farms and wildlife habitats. Roots of Peace will plant two million fruit and nut trees in Afghanistan and provide farmers there with the skills and support necessary for sustainable land use.